My Life With the Spirits

My Life
With the Spirits

A Magical Autobiography

Lon Milo DuQuette

Boston, MA/York Beach, ME

First published in 1999 by
Red Wheel/Weiser, LLC
York Beach, ME
With offices at:
368 Congress Street
Boston, MA 02210
www.redwheelweiser.com

Library of Congress Cataloging-in-Publication Data:
DuQuette, Lon Milo.
   My life with the spirits : a magical autobiography /
Lon Milo DuQuette.
      p. cm.
   Includes bibliographical references and index.
   ISBN 1-57863-120-3 (pbk : alk. paper)
   1. DuQuette, Lon Milo. 2. Magicians—United States—
Biography. I. Title.
BF1598.D86A3 1999
133.4'092—dc21
   [B]   99-20559
                                                                CIP

Typeset in 11/13 Minion
Cover design by Jody Dark Eagle Breedlove copyright © 1999

Printed in Canada

09 08 07 06 05
9 8 7 6 5 4 3

To my son, Jean-Paul Lafayette DuQuette.

Author's note: I have changed the names of many of the individuals who appear in *My Life with the Spirits* in order to respect and maintain their privacy. I have not, however, attempted to invent or consolidate characters for the sake of literary convenience.

Contents

List of Illustrations

Prologue:
Sons of the Desert

It was thirty-one years ago this morning, February 26, 1967. I was 18 years old and my brother Marc was 24. We sat atop one of the monstrous boulders that are heaped like petrified dinosaur droppings across California's Mojave desert and watched the moon bury itself in the western sands. 180 degrees away, the eastern horizon split in a lewd and blood red invocation of the sun. Shortly before this celestial orgy we shared a mystic feast of far too much LSD[1] and vowed in deadly earnest that we would not return from the wilderness until we were holy men. Daybreak found us shish kebabed to death—skewered through by the sun and moon's perfect opposition—flat on our backs emitting short grunts and giggles.

It would be an understatement to say we were naive, but we were not entirely green behind the psychedelic ears. Between the two of us we had at least two dozen carefully programmed "trips" under our belts. In our pitiful way we were serious seekers. We followed the "set-setting-guide" procedures outlined by Drs. Leary and Albert, and crammed the days and weeks between our sessions with healthy doses of Eastern Mysticism and spiritual practices.

---

[1] I think it is important for the reader to know that, while the methodical use of psychedelic substances played an important and generally positive role in my early spiritual career, I no longer use nor do I advocate the use of drugs for magical or recreational purposes.

Nothing, however, could have prepared us for judgment day at Joshua Tree. By mid-afternoon we had blithely paddled our souls up the river of our genetic ancestry, stood at the very hub of eternity, and stared with wagging jaws down the orbiting spokes of all possible possibilities. It was the most deafening of unspoken truths—we would never leave the desert. Wherever we would go, whatever we would do from that point forward would take place in the desert. Our frenzied hike back to my old VW bus was a stumbling ordeal of Odyssean scale, complete with horrifying labyrinths of dry washes and box-canyons, a blinding sandstorm and the sadistic laughter of the spirits of our own tormented childhoods.

The two-hour drive back to Costa Mesa was uneventful except for occasional highway encounters with desert skeletons returning home from church in their pickup trucks. Once home we immediately sought dark refuge in the smoky coolness of the Buccaneer, the only bar in town that would occasionally ignore the fact that I was a minor and serve me beer. That evening no one dared question my age. I looked a million years old.

The beers didn't help. We were still very high. The zebra-striped walls of the little saloon dripped down to the floor like melting wax, and the pores of the bartender's nose were so big I could walk inside them.

Then, from nowhere, I received a revelation—not a cosmic vision about DNA or the nature of light and time, but a surprisingly "normal" idea. It became very clear to me that I must marry Constance, my Nebraska high school sweetheart. That's all there was to it. I converted a few dollar bills into coins (an act of tortuous complexity that seemed to require many days) and shuffled to the old black pay phone near the pinball machine. I closed one eye and plugged the emptiness of Zero with my blue-green fingertip and spun the clicking wheel of fortune. I pleaded with the operator to help me place the call to Nebraska.

Constance answered.

After a few moments of attempting to communicate with my hands, I managed to identify myself. She sounded very happy to hear from me—after all, it was her birthday. I couldn't believe the cosmic coincidence, but concealed the fact that I didn't have a clue it was her birthday. Then I came out and said it.

"Would you like to get married?" (It was the smartest thing I would ever do.)

After a short pause she said, "Yes." (It was the stupidest thing she had ever done.)

We've been married for thirty years.[2]

And what about the Sons of the Desert? Did we really become holy men?

After a violent decade of political radicalism, arrests, alcohol and drug abuse, and two wives, Brother Marc transformed into the very model of an Eastern ascetic. A *Sant Mat* devotee, a Satsangi of the *Radha Soami* order, he practices the strict disciplines of that august sect—a combination of Hindu yoga and Seik mysticism. He wears a huge untrimmed beard and travels each year to the Punjab region of Northern India to labor and meditate at his Master's ashram. Back at home he is a chemical dependence counselor whose clients worship at the altar of his wit and wisdom. He is happily married to a beautiful and saintly woman—one of the most gifted psychics in the world—also a Satsangi.

Yes, I'd say Marc is a holy man, and I am very respectful of the spiritual direction his life has taken. I have no doubts that it is his way. It certainly rescued him from an early grave and his conversion has made Southern California a less dangerous place to live.

---

[2] Perhaps one of the reasons our marriage has been so enduring is the fact that I had the wisdom to wait until our 20th wedding anniversary to confess that I proposed to her on acid.

My life, on the other hand, took a dramatically different turn—so different in fact, that many people, perhaps even my brother, believe my chosen path to be patently evil.

It is true. I have scorned and rejected the faith of my fathers. I invoke and worship strange and terrible gods. I summon devils and hold congress with angels, spirits, and demons; but does it naturally follow that these pursuits are spiritual transgressions that bar me from the fellowship of holy ones? In this little book I search for an answer to that question.

I hope the reader will appreciate the fact that I have departed from the textbook format of some of my earlier works on magick and have nestled a great deal of technical information within narratives of my experiences. The first chapters are filled with much autobiographical material. Please forgive me if such memoirs seem at first irrelevant to the subject of magick. I assure you they are not. I firmly believe that in order for us both to understand *what I do* it will first be necessary to understand who I am and where I came from.

Magick is an art—as much an art as painting or music or dance. To understand and appreciate the artist's portfolio it is helpful, perhaps even essential, to know something of the character and motivations that drive him or her to produce a body of work. I am a practitioner of the "black art" (or so it has been called for the last two thousand years). I am a spiritual craftsman. I fashion my creations from thought and dream and will. No easel can suffer the subtle burden of such elements. They must be splashed against the canvas of my own soul. It is no more possible to gaze directly upon these objects d'art than it is to look upon the essence of my being. The most that can be done is to study the shadows they cast upon my memory.

For my silhouette studio I have been graciously allowed the tissue-thin pages of this book. The reader may wish to start at the beginning of the exhibition or leisurely wander the halls at random. I hope you enjoy your visit and will come away with a greater appreciation of your own life as a magical artist.

The gallery doors are now open, and the images of light and darkness that hang from the walls are the intangible tales of *my life with the spirits.*

CHAPTER 1

I Am Born[1]

Except for the frustration and embarrassment of incontinence, infancy was a perfectly delightful experience. Soon after I learned to walk, it was discovered that I was afflicted with Perthes' disease in my right hip. Perthes' is a serious bone malady that crumbles the topmost part of the thigh. In order to prevent complete disintegration of my hip socket the doctors ordered me off my feet and back into the crib. This was fine with me. It meant I could comfortably lounge undisturbed for many hours each day, drifting blissfully in and out of consciousness.

Unlike able-bodied children who, as soon as they begin to walk and talk, lose the precious memories of their pre-linguistic inner-life, my little brain was allowed to crystallize and permanently register those thoughts and images. As long as I was quiet,

---

[1] My brother tells me that when our parents brought me home from the hospital, the nanny who had cared for him picked me up over her head, looked into my drooling face and said, "I wonder what he was in his previous life?" My mother snatched me from her hands, called her a witch and fired her on the spot.

my mother was quite satisfied to leave me to my semi-conscious musings.

Among these were visions of myself as an adult man crouching in a dirt trench with a half a dozen other men. It was night, but the sky would brighten from time to time with brilliant explosions. Oddly enough, this image wasn't particularly frightening.

The most frequent recurring picture that projected itself upon the screen of my bedroom ceiling was triggered by the smell of night-blooming jasmine that my father had planted near my nursery window. I saw myself (again as an adult man) stepping into a car (that I would later determine was of the late 1920s or early 1930s vintage) and driving south on (what I would later discover was) the Pacific Coast Highway 101 from Santa Monica to Ensenada, Mexico.[2] The night was hot and all I could think about was the woman I was to meet there. I was in love. I physically ached to be with my lover. My infantile mind couldn't visualize what exactly I was going to do with her, but certain parts of my newly acquired baby body informed me in no uncertain terms that there were many things that could indeed be done.[3]

The reader who may be theorizing that these feelings and images were suggested by things I had seen on television or in the movies must remember that as a bed-ridden infant in 1948–1950, I had not been exposed to either medium. I am not sharing this information with you in order to prove anything about reincarnation or genetic memory. (I can't even put up a good

---

[2] In 1980 I visited a palatial old gambling casino/hotel in Ensenada built by boxer Jack Dempsey in the early 30s. I instantly recognized it as the destination of this vision.

[3] Naturally, another reward for enduring long hours of privacy was the ecstasy of physical self-discovery and experimentation. I must confess, I discovered this all-important aspect of life at a very early age and applied myself diligently. The mental images that evoked this behavior were clear, explicit, and decidedly adult.

argument for the reality of life after *birth*). I only want you to know that the overriding character of my self-identity was that of an adult trapped in an infant's body.

I still possessed the emotions of a child. I couldn't read or write—I couldn't do calculus or play the violin. I was as stupid, naive, and crabby as any child. I simply couldn't wait to grow up to feel like myself. This created a level of tension whenever I interacted with family members. I detested being patronized like a child and cursed my helpless condition. I vividly remember after one particularly agonizing event (probably relating to food or poop) vowing in passionate babbles, "I hate being a baby! If I ever grow up I'll never get myself in this position again!"

Without a doubt, the most profound of these crib meditations was an exercise I practiced daily whereby I pondered the nature of my own existence. Without the benefit of words to frame the questions, I somehow asked myself "Was I *off* before I was *on*? If I weren't who I am, who would I be?" I then tried to imagine myself not "on." I never succeeded. Each time I imagined myself switched "off," I instantly found myself switched "on" in another consciousness center—my brother, my mother, or father. or someone-anyone-else. This frustrated me no end because if there was one thing I *did* know it was that I was "I" and nobody else. Nevertheless, I played this game every day in hopes that I would someday break out of the helical loop. I finally gave up.

It was also in my crib that I was first exposed to religious propaganda. As soon as I was old enough not to eat them, my mother gave me copies of *The Upper Room*, a tiny booklet published regularly by the Methodist Church.[4] The cover of each issue displayed a famous painting depicting incidents in the life

---

[4] She may as well have given me a loaded gun to play with.

of Christ—walking on water—knocking at the door—the crucifixion—reaching for a lost lamb—the Last Supper, that sort of
thing.

At first I wanted to like this Jesus character, but I was very
disturbed by my mother's insistence that I wouldn't really get to
know him until I was dead. Moreover, she told me that he looked
down from heaven and saw everything I did. He even knew what
I was thinking. She warned me if I didn't believe in him or was
naughty that terrible things would happen to me when I died.
Jesus and his father would put me in hell, a place she described
as *a lake of fire where you'll have nightmares and never be able to
wake up*. Every night after tucking me in she "led" me in prayer—

> *Now I lay me down to sleep.*
> *I pray the Lord my soul to keep.*
> *If I should die before I wake,*
> *I pray the Lord my soul to take.*

This prayer did not comfort me at all. It was an oath I was forced
to take against my will. It terrified me and plunged me into a
nightly crisis. My *soul* was very real to me. As a person who drifted
in and out of objective consciousness all day and night, I knew
my soul to be my only *real* identity. Being a baby was humiliating enough, but the thought of this ghost-god coming down from
the clouds to steal my soul before I could grow old enough to
use the toilet was horrifying. I could not put this dreadful thought
out of my mind and sure enough, shortly after my 4th birthday,
the "Lord" would come to my bedside *my soul to take*.

CHAPTER 2

My Vision of Christ

My mother was born in 1913 in the barren sand-hills of western Nebraska. Her mother, Clara, whose ancestors fought in the American Revolution, came from sturdy Pennsylvania Dutch stock. Mom's father, Dewey, was the bastard son of the daughter of a Scottish rancher named McConnell and a full-blooded Cherokee Indian named William Lake. Great Grandfather Lake, it seems, was quite the cowboy, and made his living as a performer in traveling Wild West shows. These spectacles were very popular in the 1880s and offered some of the only employment opportunities for native Americans during that genocidal era. His specialty was Roman riding, which is the act of standing up on two galloping horses—one foot on one horse, one foot on the other. Shortly after inseminating my great grandmother he was trampled to pieces as a matinee finale.

Naturally, the shame of begetting a bastard halfbreed could not be borne by the McConnell clan, and so little Dewey was given up as soon as he was weaned. The new "mother" was an outlaw "uncle" who made ends meet by selling corn whiskey, which he illicitly distilled in a honeycomb of caves south of North Platte. My grandfather became the moonshiner's slave boy and grew to manhood tending the fires and servicing the great copper kettles and coils. Out of necessity he learned the art of the blacksmith and eventually, when he was strong enough to defy his master, moved to Hershey and set up shop. Later he would marry Clara Purbaugh and try his hand at ranching. Before they divorced they had five children: two boys—Glenn and Freeman, and three girls—Gladys, Lucinda, and Avis.

Life on the plains was unbelievably harsh, and I mean no disrespect to the memories of those poor devils who, for whatever reasons, chose to stay and breed in that unforgiving wilderness. However, the sad fact remains that by the time my mother came into the world the sand hills had petrified the souls of her people, and stripped them of all but the most primitive aspects of character. What remained was a bitter stock of petty avarice, alcoholism, incest, brutality, and guilt. Suicide was a common remedy for this prairie madness. *Gettin' saved* was the other way out.

For a few weeks after Aimee Semple McPherson and her International Church of the Four-Square Gospel Crusade came to the cattle town of Paxton, the men stayed on the wagon and the womenfolk developed attitudes. Lucinda, my teenage mother-to-be, reluctantly declined an offer to join the troop as a choir member. But she loved the colorful energy of revival and wholeheartedly surrendered to a child-like belief in that particular brand of Bible abuse.

Fortunately, in our early years, my brother Marc and I were for the most part spared direct contamination from my mother's sad and unwholesome kin. We were Southern California kids, like our dad. Our house always had electricity and indoor plumbing. Our father was a Freemason. He drilled oil wells, he'd gone to UCLA, he read books and played golf—but his story will come later.

In July of 1952 Dad sacrificed his two-week vacation, loaded up the Buick and drove us all back to Nebraska to visit Mom's relatives. I had just turned 4, and was still not permitted to walk. We took historic Route 66 part of the way. It was quite an adventure. Dad didn't like to stop the car except for gas or sleep, so when nature called Marc and I were obliged to carefully pee in a glass jar in the back seat. Mom would then fling the hot piss out the passenger side window, ignoring the fact that much of it blew back through the open back window and into our faces. I was carsick much of the time, and my poor brother became so feverishly delirious as we crossed the Arizona desert that he tearfully pleaded with Dad to stop the car so he could "sit in the shade of a jackrabbit."

The 1,500 mile trip took four days. Our destination was a genuine ghost town called Wallace. Located about fifty monotonous miles southwest of North Platte (and at least eighty years back in time), Wallace had grown like a melanoma around the loading platform of the Burlington Northern railroad. During the 1920s it was the home of nearly seven hundred hardy souls, and boasted a doctor, a dentist, a drugstore, a barbershop, hardware, sundry and grocery stores, a blacksmith shop, a movie house and a hotel. By 1952 fewer than three hundred called Wallace home.

The final leg of the trip was fifty miles of dusty gravel road and prairie grass. Eventually the pointed cap of an ancient water tower pierced the hymen of the horizon. "Wallace is a pretty little town," my father quipped. "*Wasn't it?*" Marc and I were not amused. We knew we would have no fun in Wallace.

The "business district" was a dirt street about three blocks long—a dusty arcade of deserted buildings. From any point along this shallow canyon of shells a person could look to either end of the street and see nothing but prairie. There were some signs of life: a saloon on the corner (where we would find Uncle Freeman); a barbershop directly across the street—its once colorful pole cracked and bleached in the sun; C.W. Smith's grocery store—smelling of fresh butchered meat and rotting melons; and the hotel—its second floor rooms had seen no guests since before the war, its lobby and first floor coffee shop the only place in town with ceiling fans.

On both sides of the main street (it was not named "Main Street"—none of the streets were named or numbered) was a village of remarkably well-built houses with enormous yards, ancient trees, and broken sidewalks. Electricity came late to Wallace and many of the yards still had working windmill pumps and primitive diesel generators. Every backyard had an outhouse and every basement had a coal chute.

The most prominent building in town was the old school house—a dark two-story brick monstrosity that looked more like a 19th-century foundry than a school. On the cold gray cornerstone near the great double door was chiseled the year of its erection, 1917. My mother and her brothers and sisters attended high school there in the 20s. As we drove by I could almost see in the windows the ghosts of suicidal farm boys in overalls.

"See those doors? When I was 15 they slammed shut behind me so hard that a big chunk of plaster broke loose from the ceiling and hit me right on my head." Mom pulled back the part in her silver hair to reveal a long pink scar. I didn't want to look. "They thought I was dead. I don't know how long I was out. Within two months my hair turned completely gray."

Things like that happen in Nebraska.

That night we drove twenty miles further into nowhere to have dinner at the new home of one of Mom's cousins. The "new home," we would discover, was not yet finished. As a matter of fact, only the basement had been dug and cinder-blocked. Still, like a family of grotesque prairie dogs, my kinsmen crammed their stove and other furniture into this hole in the sod and covered it all with a tarpaulin.

As Dad carried me down the creaking steps I was greeted warmly by the patriarch prairie dog who pulled my hair and said, "So this is Ronnie! This boy's too goddamned big to be carried 'round like a baby! You leave this 'un with us. He don't look like no cripple. We'll have him on his goddamned feet doin' chores in no goddamned time."

Dinner was a buffet of fatty ham, fried chicken, home-canned corn and green beans. Everything smelled like gasoline. There were at least six sunken mystery pies that reeked of lard, and a huge bowl of lime Jell-O topped with (of all things) mayonnaise. Inexplicably they called this quivering monstrosity "salad." Except for the celery stocks stuffed with browning cream cheese and grape Kool-Aid, I couldn't even look at the food.

Sensing my terror at the bill-of-fare my country cousins amused themselves by thrusting various morsels of mystery meat into my mouth when I least expected it. These simple folk never seemed to tire of the game. I eventually joined in the fun and started to cry (which I finally realized was the object of the game). Before the evening was over I became violently ill. Dad was relieved to have an excuse to leave early and bundled us into the car. As we sped back over the moonless prairie my mother pushed my head out of the car window so I wouldn't vomit on her new dress. I stared out into the clear Nebraska sky and saw for the first time in my young life the glory of the Milky Way. Sick as I was, I was transfixed. I had never seen anything like that in California. The creamy cloud of stars seemed to go on forever, like the desert, like the prairie. Suddenly the fabric of my newfound heaven was ruptured by a flaming red ball with a magnificent silver tail. I had never seen a shooting star before. It was breathtaking, but it startled me so that I reacted as if it were a personal violation, a cruel cosmic barb aimed at me. When you're sick everything irritates you. By the time we reached Aunt Gladys' house in Wallace I was out of my head with fever and had severe diarrhea.

"I know how to stop him shit'n." Aunt Gladys was an enormous woman, crippled since childhood with a disease that gelatinized her bones, but she was a diarrhea expert. It took both Dad and Uncle Guy to hold me down while the womenfolk administered the enema of cold water and cornstarch. I screamed myself unconscious trying to avoid this enlightened remedy. It had been a bad day.

When I awoke I found myself alone in a large bed in the guestroom. The room was dark and smelled like bleach, Vicks-Vapo-Rub and tobacco. The house was quiet. Everyone had gone to bed. I drifted in and out of a fever dream that found me peddling my tricycle down the main street of Wallace. Every building was alive with legions of cowboy ghosts wandering aimlessly in and out of the stores. One of them spoke to me and invited me to go upstairs to "Johnny Skeleton's mouse-house," and asked me something about "nails for the baseball game."

"Wallace is a ghost town," another voice announced. I couldn't have agreed more.

I closed my eyes and listened to the crickets and the hiss in my brain caused by fever. When I opened them again I was startled to see someone standing at the foot of my bed—not just someone—it was Jesus—standing in a long white robe, his arms slightly outstretch to his side, the bloody palms of his hands turned toward me.

I had never been so afraid in all my life. I pulled the covers over my head and mentally chanted (for I knew he could read my mind) "Please go away. I'm not dead! I just had diarrhea. Go away, please! I'm better now. Go away!"

I tried to calm myself down. "I'm having a bad dream," I told myself, "but I'm awake now. Jesus is *not* at the foot of the bed."

Slowly I pulled back the covers from over one eye. Still there! Jesus was *still* there! I dove, this time more deeply, beneath the covers. I was burning with fever. *Hell is a lake of fire where you have nightmares and can never wake up.* I wanted more than anything to be home in my own bed, in my own cool house in California. Jesus wouldn't dare come to California to get me. He needed enemas and ghosts and outhouses and long pink scars and fatty meat and Jell-O with mayonnaise to be God.

I don't know how many times I plunged under the suffocating covers. Each time I resurfaced Jesus was still there waiting patiently for *my soul to take.* My fear turned into panic and then into hate. I hated Jesus. I hated my relatives and all grownups who believed in this monster and made him real. If I were grown up, if I were strong, I could make him go away, but I'm a weak little kid. It wasn't fair. What kind of God terrorizes little kids when they're sick? Why did I ever invite him to take my soul?

Finally, exhaustion and lack of oxygen prevailed, and I drifted into unconsciousness with my head buried under the sweat-soaked pillows. I would not awaken until the cheeping of sparrows told me the sun was up. The morning light gave me courage to confront my terror. I threw the pillows and covers off my face and sat straight up.

Jesus was gone. In his place, my mother's yellow dress hung neatly from the closet door.

CHAPTER 3

I Die

As every holy man will tell you, in order to be spiritually born again it is first necessary to spiritually die. I have died more times than I care to remember—but never of natural causes. Anybody can die of natural causes. When you die by natural causes you stay dead. In order to be born again you must die by your own hand or be murdered.

The first time I recall being murdered was on the morning of my 5th birthday, July 11, 1953. My assassins conspired in whispers the kitchen. I heard my mother tell my brother, "He's 5 now. Christmas is five months away. It's best to do it now, not close to Christmas. You tell him. You can do it nicely. He'll be okay when all those kids come for his birthday party."

Marc was a dear soul. He was tall for 11 and had the habit of chewing on his shirt collar when he was nervous (which was nearly all the time). He came into the den where I had been eavesdropping. We sat down on Dad's big chair. He stuck his collar in his mouth.

"You know Santa Claus?"

"Yeah."

"Santa Claus isn't real, he's..."

"Yes he is!" I cut him off before he said anything else. I pushed my tiny palms against his lips trying to shove the words back in his mouth. "I sat on his lap. Mom's got a picture. He gave me my paint box at your school show. He knew my name."

"Those are guys in Santa Claus costumes."

"Shut up! He's real!" I started to cry. "You're saying this to be mean to me on my birthday."

"No I'm not."

"He comes. He eats the cookies. He drinks the milk. He leaves all those things for us."

"Mom and Dad wait 'til we're asleep. Then they get up and eat the cookies. They drink the milk, and they buy all that stuff for us themselves—other people buy us stuff too, and say it's from Santa. He's just a pretend guy and big kids all know he's not real. You don't want the big kids to make fun of you, do you?"

I was beginning to realize he was telling me the truth. I could easily imagine such a black secret bubbling in the heart of an evil "big kid."

"He is *too* real!" By now I was lying to myself. I kept crying just to hear myself cry. They were my last little kid tears. I knew when I stopped I would be a big kid and there would be no more magic in the world.

"It's okay, we'll always get stuff on Christmas morning." Marc was as sweet a brother as anyone could ask for.

"There's no Easter Bunny either, is there?"

"Nope."

"And when I put my teeth under the pillow..."

"Mom takes your tooth while you're asleep and puts a nickel there."

I didn't have to ask the next question and he didn't have to tell me. We just sat quietly in Dad's big chair until I stopped crying.

Jesus isn't real either, I thought. He's just a yellow dress.

CHAPTER 4

I Descend Into Hell

My father was born on November 11th, 1911, in a house at 1111 11th Street in Los Angeles. The midwife who attended his birth was so impressed by the array of elevens that, even though the time of birth was afternoon, she logged the time of birth as 11:11 A.M. She hoped it would bring the child luck. It did not. He had one sister and three half-sisters, all older than he.

Dad's father, Joseph Oliver DuQuette, was a brooding and eccentric Frenchman who came to America in 1899. He was a barber by trade and a self-taught scholar by passion. He spoke seven languages fluently. He once told my father he never dreamed in the same language two nights in a row. This gift of tongues was a valuable asset for one who scraped the chins of the huddled immigrant masses. The sign in the window of his Long Beach emporium proudly announced (in their respective vernaculars) "French, Italian, German, Greek, Portuguese, Spanish, and English spoken here." He was an insatiable reader, and by 1928 could boast that he had read every book in the great Long Beach Central Library.

Joseph's tendency to overachieve may have been an attempt to compensate for a singular physical shortcoming. Childhood malnutrition and pre-adolescent drinking and smoking ensured that he would never grow taller than four feet six inches. Before his death in 1938 he was prone to severe bouts of depression, sometimes locking himself in his room for days with only a chamber pot, books, and wine.

Shortly after Joseph arrived in New York from France, he met and married Jessie Harland, an Englishwoman and the widowed mother of three girls. Her husband, so she told Joseph, had fallen ill during the crossing and died before reaching New York. Ironically, he was not the only man in her life to be taken by the cruel Atlantic. Her father, a Scotland Yard inspector, died in a similar manner returning from Canada where he had been helping with the security arrangements for Queen Victoria's visit. What started as a sniffle and cough in Ottawa on the second day out quickly turned to pneumonia. He was dead before the ship docked.

Joseph, Jessie, and the three girls (Beatrice, Marge, and little Jessie), moved to Los Angeles in 1904. They would have two children together, Vina and my father, Clifford. All his sisters called him "Bud."

Although Joseph ridiculed the church, he enrolled the children in Catholic school. Little Bud grew to be quite an athlete. Gymnastics and track and field were his great passion. He competed in a handful of regional and national events and finished with respectable times. He briefly dreamed of Olympic competition but would soon awaken to the realities of his family's poverty. After high school he found work as a roughneck in the Signal Hill oil fields and married every woman he slept with.

Throat cancer claimed Grandpa Joseph in 1938 while my father was wildcatting for oil in Kansas and Nebraska. The family made no attempt to contact him with the news, and he didn't bother to write them to announce that he married again. This time the bride was a waitress from Ogalala, NE by the name of Lucinda Myrtle McConnell. Dad didn't find oil in the sand hills, and in 1940, he and Lucinda returned to California. His mother died just a few months after meeting her new daughter-in-law. She was interred at Sunnyside Mausoleum in Long Beach. Dad's sisters would never tell him where his father was buried.

All the characters of this American drama were dead by the time I was born except my father and aunts Vina and Beatrice. The sisters never visited us, even though they lived only a few miles away. They despised my mother and wallowed in a hateful feud spawned at the foot of their mother's deathbed—something about the final disposition of furniture or silverware or some other pitiful scraps of the poor woman's possessions.

In 1955, after twenty-five years of toiling in the oil-soaked dust of the Huntington Beach oil fields, Dad announced that he wanted to quit his job and start his own water well drilling business. An eight-year drought in the midwest was making millionaires of the few savvy drillers who were turning the great plains green with shallow ground water. To my utter disbelief and terror, he told us we would be moving to Nebraska. I would have been happier had he announced he was going to kill me.

Sensing our panic, Dad assured Marc and me we would not be living in Wallace or anywhere near Mom's relatives. As a matter of fact, we would be making our home in Columbus—in Eastern Nebraska over two hundred miles from Wallace, in the rich green pastureland between the Platte and Loop rivers. The Pawnee Indians called this land the "happy hunting grounds." Not only would there be lots of trees there, but in the wintertime we could play in the snow! (Mom told me it tasted like whipped cream.) We would be living in a real town with paved streets, indoor toilets and supermarkets with electric-eye doors. It wouldn't be anything like Wallace.

I still had my doubts. I loved Southern California. My hip was getting better and I was allowed to walk with crutches. If all continued to go well I would be on my feet in a year or two. I was just starting to live. We visited the beach often and the radio was filled with hip new music that could only be heard in California called "no-named-jive." I loved it. I just knew there wasn't any corner of Nebraska where they had ever heard of Johnny Otis or the Three Tons of Joy.

It was December by the time we sold the house. Because the new owners wanted to take occupancy a few weeks before we were ready to leave, we spent our last California Christmas in an ancient motel in Belmont Shores. On the eve of our departure Dad made a horrifying announcement. Our new house in Columbus would not be ready for us to occupy until March. We would have to go first to Wallace and live with Aunt Gladys until spring. Marc and I would have to attend school for at least three months in that prehistoric building that attacked my mother and turned her hair gray. Our Christmas gifts were snowboots, parkas, and gloves.

The winter in Wallace was very difficult. I was immediately enlightened regarding the taste of snow. My schoolmates were as course and cruel as their environment and they tormented me over my crutches and everything I said, did, or wore, that was un-Nebraskan. (I couldn't understand why they called lunch "dinner" and they called dinner "supper.") The worst frustration resulted from the huge disparity between the California and Nebraska school systems. Nebraska was far more advanced than California in the lower grades, and I immediately found myself at least two years behind in math and English. I was completely lost and did not have a clue how to catch up. I never did.

Every school day became simply an exercise in survival. Mom wouldn't let me voice my complaints in the presence of her relatives, who were kind enough to put us up that miserable winter. It wouldn't have done any good anyway. I cheered myself with the thought that spring would come and we would move to a real town with paved streets, indoor toilets and supermarkets with electric-eye doors.

✠   ✠   ✠

"Welcome the First Day of Spring." The words were written in colorful pastel colors across the top of the blackboard. The board itself was covered with an incredibly beautiful chalk mural—scores of flowers, bunnies, squirrels, bees, and baby birds in a nest, all dominated by a huge yellow sun. I had never seen anything like it. Miss Shoemaker was a great artist. I was in love with her. She must have stayed up all night to draw it.

This was the day I dreamed of those dreadful months in Wallace. Columbus wasn't California, but it was at least fifty years ahead of Wallace. The weather on the first day of spring did not match Miss Shoemaker's colorful drawing. It was four degrees below zero and the third day of a blinding blizzard. The streets were impassable so I trudged my way through the drifts to school. I was in the second grade and totally lost in all my subjects except one—music. I learned I could sing. Nobody was more surprised than I. For the ten years I remained in Nebraska, my musical abilities and my service in the Methodist church would be the only skills I would need to survive.

CHAPTER 5

Altar Boy

"Lonnie! Do you believe in Jesus?" Rev. Alan Castner squeezed the new black Bible in both hands like it was an overstuffed sandwich. That Bible was mine. I earned it. I squirmed through two tedious years of Sunday School and survived the most obscene and evil form of legalized child abuse ever devised—Vacation Bible School. I passed their examinations. I got up before dawn every Sunday to sing in the children's choir at early service. On Saturday mornings while my friends were playing army or watching Sky King on TV, I sat alone in the musty and haunted hundred-year-old chapel and mindlessly folded the next day's bulletins and responsive readings.

Did *I* believe in Jesus? Didn't I dress up like a cherub each Sunday and march down the aisle bearing the sacred flame? Didn't I start each 11:00 A.M. service by enkindling the massive candles upon the altar that signified the living presence of God? And who was it that ended each service by solemnly extinguishing the candles with the long brass snuffer? Me, that's who!

Did I believe in Jesus? Did *I* believe in Jesus?

Hell no! I didn't believe in Jesus! But I earned that goddamned Bible! Now, standing before the altar of God, in front of my parents and the entire congregation, I was going to have to lie to get it.

"Yes sir."

I was 9 years old and at last a full-fledged Christian.

Rev. Alan looked like he was going to cry. He handed me my prize and put his hand on my shoulder and turned me toward the congregation.

"How old are you Lonnie?"

"9."

"Do you say your prayers at night?"

"Yes sir." This was not a lie for I prayed fervently every night, but not to Jesus, not to God. Each night as I stared out my window into the beautiful Nebraska sky I tearfully prayed to space aliens or any superior intelligence in the universe who could hear my plea. "Get me out of Nebraska! Take me back to California. Take me anywhere. You can perform medical experiments on me—I don't care! Just get me out of here!"

"Friends, this is our candle lighter, Lonnie DuQuette. You may not recognize him without his little white gown"—laughter—"and his torch and snuffer"—more laughter. Lonnie also sings in the Carol Choir and comes in on Saturdays to fold our bulletins. We're all sure he's going to grow to be a man of God." He then gently pushed me back toward my pew with a hearty "God bless you Lonnie."

What the dear man didn't know was that, even though I was the virginal innocent who started and ended each service, I seldom stayed to hear his sermons. Each Sunday after lighting the candles at the 11:00 o'clock service, I rushed back to the vestry, stripped out of my chasuble and slipped out the side door. With my Timex strapped tightly to my impious wrist I ran at top speed across the street, past the ancient bandstand and towering elms in Frankfort Square, straight to the soda fountain of Tooley's drug store. There, after catching my breath, I lingered over my own Eucharist—a tuna salad sandwich (with an unforgettable home-canned bread-n-butter pickle) and a cherry phosphate. I knew what heaven was. After my sandwich I had just enough time to browse a comic book or two before rushing back to church to close the service.

I paid for this weekly orgy with the winnings from a weekly crap game I organized before Sunday school in the church basement. My father had been kind enough to teach me the rules to this venerable game and I easily attracted a pool of easy marks—their pockets bulging with cash that would otherwise be destined for the offering plate. Predictably, the game was finally raided and my "bones" confiscated by George Sorensen, a racist construction mogul and spiritual exhibitionist who had bullied his way into the position of Sunday School Headmaster.

Each week before the individual classes adjourned to their respective cells, he "taught" the general assembly of all the grades in the large common room. Here we drank deeply from the fountain of his bigoted wisdom, learning why people who lived before Jesus (including Adam, Eve, Abraham, and Socrates) were burning in Hell, and why Blacks had to work for white people because Noah's grandson saw him naked.

On the morning of my arrest he strutted to the front of the assembly and held up my precious green dice in front of all the students and bellowed, "These evil dice was brung into God's house by one of your own classmates to steal God's money. I bet he thinks it's real funny. I tell ya one thing, God don't think it's funny. I ain't gonna tell you who done this. He knows who he is, and God knows who he is."

Then with a dramatic sweep of his hand he hurled the dice into the trashcan and added dramatically, "All I can say is—I'll pray for him."

As much as I despised George-*if-their-religion-won't-let-'em-eat-cows-why-don't-them-godless-Hindus-start-eatin-all-them-*

monkeys-they-got-jumpin-around-India-Sorensen, I loved Reverend Alan. I admired his youthful enthusiasm and positive attitude. He had a beautiful young wife and I fantasized what life must be like in the rectory. He preached no hell-fire and made it seem like it should be fun to be a Methodist whether you believed in God or not. I was so comfortable with his brand of religion that (even though I was a secret unbeliever) I told my parents I wanted to be a Methodist minister when I grew up. Even my freethinking father attended service each week to show his support for this dynamic man who was sent by the bishop to build our new church.

He built the new church all right. Predictably, the building contractor was George-if-they-ain't-been-baptized-then-they're-burnin-in-Hell-even-if-they-are-just-little-babies-Sorensen. Unfortunately, before erection of the new church was completed his 12-year-old daughter walked in on him playing Adam & Eve with Reverend Alan's wife in the new church annex. The scandal shocked the town and forced the Castners to move away.[1]

My father stopped going to church. I continued to serve under the next pastor and the next one and the next. After a short vacation George Sorensen resumed his job as Sunday School Headmaster.

All I can say is—I'll pray for him.

---

[1] In a midnight raid, my brother, Marc, and two of his high school friends salted the lawn of the pious church board member who was most instrumental in forcing the Castners to leave town. A summer rain later that night assured the soil was ruined to a depth of six feet. A few days later we rode our bicycles past what looked like a swimming pool being dug in his front yard.

CHAPTER 6

Holy Communion

When I was 11, I graduated to the adult chorus, first as a so-prano then later as second tenor. I continued to sing in the church choir until I graduated from high school and moved back to California. I hated it, but I had no choice.

At age 7, I made a Faustian pact with Robert M. Carlton, the brilliant and tyrannical director of the vocal music department of the high school and the undisputed *Kapellmeister* of the entire school district. His ensembles and one-hundred-ten voice Master Chorale consistently won state and regional awards and the honors he brought to our provincial town year after year made him as feared and respected among the faculty and alumni as any winning football coach. He also directed the Methodist Church adult choir.

I sang in school and church choruses under his direction from the second grade until after high school graduation. He was not a likable man. He yelled. He was cruel and utterly insensitive to the feelings of others. He made children cry. He suffered migraines, and the blade of his wit was always wet with the blood of his inferiors, and everybody was his inferior. I have no idea why he singled me for out special treatment from among the other reluctant warblers, but single me out he did. From sixth grade through my senior year he gave me the choicest slots in recitals and the leads in the seasonal shows and musicals.

He never told me I had to sing in the church choir. He didn't have to. After all, for my entire high school career he personally bullied and threatened all my other teachers to assure that I maintained a C-plus average in all my classes. If my grades were to drop below C-plus I would not be allowed to participate in the various performances throughout the year. He made sure that never happened and I was shamelessly impudent in my security.[1] I was the classic class clown. I never took a book home, seldom passed a test and even though I was punished by a detention period every day without exception for three consecutive years (a school record), I maintained a C-plus average.

Shortly after I turned 14 my musical career expanded when I was asked to join a local garage band. I played guitar like most boys my age, but what drew me to the attention of my much older colleagues was the fact that I hosted an after-school radio program on the local AM station and might be

---

[1] I was expelled from high school on two occasions: the first time in my Junior year because my hair was too long, and once in my Senior year for "seditious activity on campus" (a charge relating to my involvement with the Students for a Democratic Society and the anti-war movement). I was reinstated on the former occasion at the intervention of Mr. Carlton who pointed out to the School Board that I was a professional musician (who needed a longhair image) and my family needed my support because of my father's terminal illness. The charge of "seditious activity on campus" was dropped and I was reinstated when a local Episcopal minister (a friend in the anti-war movement and a member of the American Civil Liberties Union) intervened on my behalf.

able to provide free advertising for the band. It was also nice that I knew the words to nearly every popular song recorded since 1952.

To everyone's surprise our little band worked regularly, playing proms and sockhops in small towns throughout Nebraska and all neighboring states. Our success was largely due to the efforts of our 25-year-old bass player. I made a point of jotting down the names and phone numbers of everyone who ever booked us and a year later I formed my own band, "The Panics." We were pretty good and stayed together until I completed high school.

In the spring of 1966 the years of my indentured service to Mr. Carlton were drawing to an end. Thanks to his powers of coercion I knew I would graduate from high school (college prep no less). With the help of my brother (who had returned to California the moment he finished high school six years earlier) I made arrangements to move to Costa Mesa to attend college. Almost out of nostalgia I showed up at the church for the last few choir rehearsals and Sunday performances. The last Methodist ceremony I would ever attend was a most memorable communion service.

Eschewing pagan ritual and not wishing to be confused with the Satanic Church of Rome, Methodists, like most Protestants, take communion infrequently. What is for Catholics the central and most intensely personal act of worship is to Protestants an embarrassing reminder that once upon a time in order to be a Christian it was necessary to regularly put one's faith where one's mouth was and then swallow it.

Methodists take pride in the fact they don't believe a priest is necessary to ritualistically bless and consecrate the sacred elements. They don't believe that words (Latin or otherwise) can conjure the Holy Spirit into the blessed cup. They don't believe that common bread and wine can be magically transubstantiated into the flesh and blood of God. As a matter of fact, where the sacrament of communion is concerned, Protestants just don't believe.

Nonetheless, like island natives who in obedience to some primitive instinct still fling an occasional virgin into a volcano, they set aside a handful of Sundays a year to pass around plates piled high with tiny cubes of Wonderbread and microscopic glasses of grape juice, and eat and drink when ordered to do so.

On that last Sunday the subject of the sermon was "The Lonely Atheist." As I slouched half-awake in the choir loft—my hormones roaring uncontrollably to the sweet memory of Saturday night's backseat embraces—something else (almost as profound) was rising beneath my purple choir robe. Realization. Suddenly I *realized* that I was at peace with my atheism. Ever since the Santa Claus revelation I had been cynically convinced of the non-existence of the God of the Bible, but the severity of my earlier programming and my subsequent life in the church coated me with a waxy film of residual doubts. That bright morning, without any known catalyst or undue introspection, all doubts simply evaporated. Suddenly I became deliriously comfortable with the simple fact that all of it, even atheism, is bullshit. I almost laughed out loud.

I realize this doesn't sound like much of a revelation, but at that moment it tickled me ecstatically. I never felt so liberated in my life. I looked up at the enormous circular stained glass window behind the altar and could almost hear the "Hallelujah Chorus." How profoundly appropriate it was that this revelation should occur in church, for this is the secret, I concluded, of all religions: There is no God! There is no God, and it really doesn't matter!

I looked around at the restless and coughing congregation and smugly wallowed in the luxury of feeling sorry for these frightened sheep. I *did* feel a bit like a hypocrite sitting there with the choir, lending my unbelieving voice to a meaningless worship service. Still, I thought, it was a job. I owed it to Mr.

Carlton. But then I remembered it was Communion Sunday. Oh no you don't! Never again. I really would be a hypocrite if I took part in that absurd act of mock cannibalism. I decided I would sit this one out. It would be my declaration of liberation. I couldn't wait to *not* take communion.

The sermon wound to a dreary conclusion. "Can you imagine how lonely you would be if you had only yourself to look to?" Dr. Petty then announced we would now commemorate the "Lord's Supper." Mr. Carlton stood up and indicated to the choir to rise. The choir was to take communion first. My place was in the very middle of the tenor section. I had people on both sides of me. I couldn't remain seated. I was trapped into filing out with everybody else. "Damn it!" I thought. "Now I will have to stand there while everyone kneels to take communion. Dr. Petty will probably look at me and wait until I kneel. I might have to say something. It will be incredibly awkward."

I toyed with the idea of just marching out the side door and running to Tooley's for a tuna sandwich, but the thought of Mr. Carlton's wrath made me reconsider. I decided to go to the rail with the choir, kneel down like everybody else, but when the time came to communicate I would just kneel there respectfully. My back would be turned to the congregation. No one would notice except perhaps Dr. Petty and he wouldn't say anything until after church. It might even be an interesting conversation.

Mr. Carlton was more than a choir director. He was a puppet master. He conducted through a rich vocabulary of subtle body language and his singers never took their eyes off him. Barely moving two fingers he compelled us like so many marionettes to parade to the communion rail and line up shoulder to shoulder. He then dropped us to our knees in perfect unison with an almost imperceptible nod of his head. We knelt there in our long robes like a row of purple tents.

I was very excited, or maybe a little scared. My heart pounded so loudly I could hear it clicking in my mouth.

> *Now on the evening He was betrayed, as they were eat-*
> *ing, Jesus took bread, and blessed, and broke it, and gave*
> *it to the disciples and said, "Take, eat. For this is my*
> *body."*

Everybody took and ate. I took not. I ate not. It was my first
adult act of conscience. I swooned with ecstasy. I had never felt
so alive in my life.

> *And when they had eaten he took a cup, and when*
> *he had given thanks he gave it to them, saying "Drink*
> *of it, all of you; for this is my blood of the covenant,*
> *which is poured out for many for the forgiveness of*
> *sins."*

Everybody took and drank. I took not. I drank not. I was almost
hyperventilating. I felt I would burst.

> *And he said to them; "I tell you I shall not drink again*
> *of this fruit of the vine until that day when I drink it*
> *new with you in my Father's kingdom."*

It was over in just a moment. The others downed their pathetic
drop of grape juice and returned the sticky little glasses to their
tight little holes. I had done it. I had freed myself of God. I was
one with the likes of Thomas Paine, Burtrand Russell, and Mark
Twain!

It was now time for the choir to return to the loft to ser-
enade the bovine queue of believers through their snack. We
looked to the dark eyes of Mr. Carlton and waited for his silent
permission to rise. He gave the command by raising his chin ever
so slightly while lifting his eyebrows in subtle mockery as if he
were watching angels rising to heaven.

Getting up from a kneeling position is never easy and I was
very conscious of the fact that I could inadvertently "moon" the

congregation from this position if I wasn't careful—for a sophisticated freethinker like me that would never do. I leaned back slightly and slid my left foot forward until it rested flat next to my right knee which was still planted solidly on the floor. I placed both hands on my left knee and transferred my weight to that axis and tried to rise up on my left leg. Unbeknownst to me, however, was the fact that the hem of my choir robe was pinned firmly to the floor by the toe of my right shoe. I was only able to rise two or three inches before my own robe trapped me in a most humiliating kowtow. Again I tried to rise but only managed to reach a painful stoop. My ecstasy instantly turned to panic. I couldn't even raise my head. The rest of the choir members were already on their feet. Again and again I was forced to my knees but no matter how I repositioned myself I could not free my robe from the tent-stake of my own foot. The congregation started to murmur, then giggle.

I tried again. This time when I reached the limit of my constraint I forced myself to hop violently like a one-legged hunchback two or three times in tiny jerks. At the crest of each hop I tried to lift my right foot. Each time as I landed I belched out a pitiful little grunt. This ridiculous maneuver resulted in the almost impossible act of kicking my own ass with the heel of my right foot. I was so embarrassed that I thought I would ignite. Eventually, this grotesque dance enabled me to pull myself free.

Like a tightly strung bow that suddenly had its string severed, my body sprang to attention. I was upright for only a split second before my momentum hurled me off balance and backwards towards the first row of pews. All I could see was the blur of the great stained glass window as my head snapped back violently. I knew I was toppling into humiliation and injury. As I plunged backward into the abyss, the high vaulted ceiling of the church reverberated with the only words my spasming nervous system would permit my body to release.

"Oh God!" I screamed at the top of my lungs.

CHAPTER 7

California Dreamin'

A couple of weeks after my humiliation at the communion rail I packed up my VW bus and drove as fast as I could out of Nebraska. The long nightmare was over and my future beckoned to me from golden California. I knew everything would change but I had no way of knowing how much.

The world in 1966 was far more interesting than college. I studied very little. As a drama major I soon discovered I could get through most of my classes by simply *acting* like a college student. I was just happy to be back home in California. It was everything I remembered and more. Almost immediately I found work in the evenings singing "folk music" in local saloons. I had more audacity than ability, and was so entirely unconscious of my own lack of talent that I sometimes fooled other people as well. Among them were the owners of some of the most famous folk clubs in the country including Huntington Beach's famed Golden Bear, where I twice found myself opening act for my idol, Hoyt Axton.

Soon I was befriended by other local musicians. Foremost among these was a fellow Midwesterner, Charley D. Harris, who had just returned from a successful stint in Hawaii. Charley was ten years older than I and had already made almost every mistake a young musician could make.[1] He was ready to settle down and get serious about songwriting. I convinced him to allow me to collaborate with his efforts.

We were remarkably prolific and soon produced a respectable portfolio of songs which, if I say so myself, we presented quite well. Charley had a great voice and our harmonies were very tight. This combination of skills got us through several doors in the Hollywood publishing world and earned us a measure of local notoriety. I wallowed in my local stardom. I was very poor, but life was sweet.

Like most musicians, I smoked a little grass and waxed philosophical with my colleagues over midnight steak and eggs (Man, did you like ever notice that dog spelled backwards is G-o-d?), but spirituality was the farthest thing from my mind. LSD would change that.

I dropped my first hit with a fellow musician in the men's room of a Belmont Shores blues club. It was my friend's first trip also. Once safely back in his apartment, he went into the bedroom, closed the door and remained there. I flopped down on the living room floor and for the next six hours repeatedly picked myself apart and put myself back together.

Don't worry, I won't bore the reader with another "I saw God on acid" story. It's not like that at all. It's more like an "I introduced myself to myself" story. I discovered that "myself" was an infinitely greater thing than I had ever imagined, and realized with technicolor certitude that understanding myself was going to be the only endeavor in life worth pursuing.

---

[1] He was saving a few he could make with me.

By daybreak the doors of perception had closed enough for me to put on my shoes and walk across town to my own apartment. Everything looked very different. Trees and shrubs radiated luminous auras. Telephone and power lines were coiled round with bright red and green magnetic bands. The visual effects were dazzling but no longer a wondrous distraction. My mind was focused on one joyous revelation. Everything that everybody is looking for in religion is already inside their own heads. There's no reason to *believe* anything. There's no reason to pray to anything. It can all be experienced. It *must* all be experienced. That is what we are here to do.

I encouraged my brother Marc to join me on my next "trip" about a ten days later and we found that we communicated very well while under the influence. In the weeks that followed we read everything that we could get our hands on about LSD and the psychedelic phenomenon. Almost every article compared the experience to the ecstatic visions of eastern mystics and primitive shamans. I haunted the Eastern Philosophy section of my college library and indiscriminately skimmed through anything I thought might show me where to start my holy quest. Marc began investigating yoga and the various yoga institutions in Southern California.

We put ourselves on an experimental vegetarian diet and started "practicing" the physical exercises from Swami Vishnudevananda's illustrated book of Hatha Yoga.[2] We weren't bad. Both of us were surprisingly limber and could sit in a full lotus for (what we considered) quite a long time. I could even stand on my head in a full lotus position and demand "Someone quick! Take my picture!"

---

[2] Swami Vishnudevananda, *The Complete Illustrated Book of Yoga*, Juliean Press, Inc. 1960 Library of Congress Catalog Card # 59-15568.

Quick! Take my picture!

At first we thought we could mix psychedelics and yoga. Like idiots we registered for an all day Christmas meditation at Paramahansa Yogananda's Self-Realization Fellowship Temple. In order to make sure we would get the maximum spiritual impact from the day, Marc baked the most extraordinary loaf of marijuana banana bread. It was the first time we ever tried this recipe,[3] so we were unsure how it would affect us. It was very tasty, so delicious in fact that we couldn't believe that it could be very potent. Just minutes prior to entering the Temple we sat in the car and gorged ourselves on the whole loaf.

---

[3] As I recall he soaked an entire "lid" of cleaned grass in tequila. When the tequila evaporated he then blended the paste with a pound of melted butter. After allowing it to harden he then used the loaded butter in a standard banana bread recipe.

We were warmly welcomed by a serene looking monk who ushered us to the meditation room. In the East was a small altar displaying portraits of the line of SRF gurus.[4] Facing the altar were five or six rows of straight-backed wooden chairs with padded seats. A neatly folded blanket hung over the back of each chair.

"Do we have to sit in these chairs?" I asked with affected humility. "We would prefer to sit on the floor in our asana."

The monk looked at us incredulously.

"My friends, this is an eight hour meditation. I am sure you will be more comfortable seated in chairs for that amount of time."

"We'll be the judge of that," Marc replied with a patronizing giggle.

We couldn't understand why the monk didn't believe we preferred to meditate on the floor with our legs locked in a full lotus position like real yogis.

"What kind of yogis are these?" Marc thought. (By now the banana bread was taking effect and I could read his mind.)

"Yeah!" I answered mentally. "He must think we are some kind of white guys!"

The monk showed us where we could sit on the floor and informed us there would be a break in 2¹/₂ hours in case we wanted to move to chairs at that time.

"We'll be fine," I assured him.

Within a few minutes the little chapel was filled with neatly dressed devotees. None of them elected to join the two *real* yogis on the floor. The monk said a few words about Christmas being a very spiritual season and quoted a little from the writings of Yogananda. Then we all chanted a few of the Order's "cosmic

---

[4] A year or so later pictures of these same gurus would flank the face of Aleister Crowley on the album cover of the Beatles' *Sergeant Pepper's Lonely Hearts Club Band.*

chants" and settled in for the first 2¹/₂ hour period of silent meditation.

Marc and I immediately realized that it was a big mistake to have eaten all of the banana bread. We were painfully high. We turned to one another and looked helplessly at each other's bulging yellow eyes and mentally screamed "We gotta get out of here!"

Nevertheless, we closed our eyes and tried to be troopers. Our legs soon fell asleep, and without the distraction of pain so did I. I guess I was snoring pretty loudly when Marc jabbed me in the ribs with his elbow. The monk opened one eye and silently glowered at us. It was absolutely amazing. We could read *his* mind, too!

We squirmed and dozed through the longest 2¹/₂ hours of our lives and quietly slithered to the car during the first break. We would not return to finish the meditation.

For the next few months psychedelic experiments would remain the centerpiece of our spiritual exploration. The dramatic events of our day in Joshua Tree would be the culmination of this period.

✠   ✠   ✠

Constance left Nebraska and came to live with me on June 15th, 1967. The sweet distractions of our honeymoon prevented us from accompanying Marc and a nice young Quaker couple named Karl and Elsa to a peace demonstration on June 23rd in Los Angeles. This event would have a profound effect upon Marc and change all our lives dramatically.

President Johnson was to appear at the Century Plaza Hotel in Los Angeles. It was the perfect opportunity for the Southern California peace movement to mobilize the most massive demonstration to date against the continuing escalation of the war in Vietnam. The movement on the West Coast was made up primarily of young white adult students, teachers, the clergy, and liberal professionals of the JFK/RFK ilk. The day started with the festive, love-in atmosphere that had characterized earlier L.A. demonstrations. The crowd was composed of well-dressed young couples pushing baby carriages and spectacled college types in blue work-shirts and corduroy jackets. Before sunset these dilettantes would become violently committed political radicals.

Everyone expected the scenario to follow that of previous demonstrations. The demonstrators would position themselves in front of the hotel and chant as long and as loud as possible for the benefit of the television news crews. The police would eventually give the order to disperse, everyone would boo and hiss for a few minutes and then return to their cars feeling defiantly self-satisfied.

This day would be different. Two lines of riot-equipped officers sandwiched the entire assembly in front of the hotel. When the order came to disperse, the demonstrators were prevented from moving by the line of officers behind. The officers in front of the hotel were ordered to advance on the crowd and use their batons on anyone who would not move. At the same time the police in back of the demonstrators were ordered to use their batons on anyone attempting to move back. For twenty-five bloody minutes the police clubbed away in a shameful attempt to make sure every demonstrator got a taste of the baton.

News bureaus around the country called it the worse police riot since the 1930s. Witnesses said it was a miracle nobody died at the scene. Scores were seriously injured and hospitalized. Marc was beaten on the head and face and returned home with his glasses broken and his clothes covered in blood. Karl and Elsa were also bruised and bloodied, their Quaker commitment to non-violence severely shaken.

The events of June 23, 1967 instantly polarized the political consciousness of Southern California. Moderate Democrats became ultra-liberals, ultra-liberals became radicals, and radicals became communists. Shocked by the brutality, but steadfast in their patriotism, moderate Republicans became conservatives, conservatives became ultra-nationalists, and ultra-nationalists became fascists. No one, it seemed, could remain moderate or neutral.

The horrifying reality of the war in Vietnam, and the increasingly brutal and repressive domestic environment had a curious effect on the spiritual life of our little circle of family and friends. As the chaos escalated so did our efforts toward self-discovery. We engaged in an almost desperate struggle to quickly gain enlightenment. We believed it would be our only avenue of escape from the coming holocaust.

Constance and I were married in November and I simply stopped going to college. Karl and Elsa invited us to come live with them and their four children in the suburban college community of Irvine. Karl taught Mathematics and Computer Science at the University of California, Irvine, and Elsa, a Vassar College graduate, was a professional midwife. We became the neighborhood's token "hippies" and were instantly embraced by the local liberal establishment yearning to breathe "hip." By day, Constance babysat and I gave guitar lessons. By night, Karl and Elsa hosted sumptuous sit-on-the-floor banquets where we would introduce the neighbors to marijuana, Alan Watts, Ravi Shankar, recorded Tibetan chants, and "electronic" music.

In March of 1968 we started shopping for a larger home out in the nearby canyons and forests where we could establish a private communal base. We didn't want to move too far away from Karl's job at the University. On April 4th our plans changed. The assassination of Martin Luther King plunged us into a state of tangible paranoia. Timothy Leary was advising folks to "tune in, turn on, and drop out." We were already well tuned in and turned on, nothing remained now but to drop out.

The subculture grapevine was humming with tales of utopian life in Southern Oregon. We heard of a magical place called Takilma, a tiny village on the Illinois River near the California border where land was cheap and the valley was filled with beautiful people *just like us*. There was even a mysterious wizard, a French Canadian pranic healer and follower of Yogananda who lived in a renovated barn by the river, and he was selling property next to his.

This sounded too good to ignore. Marc and Karl made an exploratory trip and determined that Takilma would be our Shangri-La. Before returning they rented a large house for us on Waldo Road near the Takilma community. The Waldo house had electricity and indoor plumbing and would afford us the opportunity to wean ourselves from urbane luxuries before we plunged completely into the primitive world of rural hippiedom. Our plan was to headquarter there until each couple could buy land that would be suitable for building our own cabins.

On May Morn, after selling nearly everything we had except guitars and books, Constance and I set out for Takilma along with Marc, his wife Margaret, Karl and Elsa, their four children and thirteen cats. There we hoped to build our own homes and live quiet lives of fasting, meditation, and study. There we intended to achieve perfect illumination before the world blew apart.

CHAPTER 8

Samadhi on Waldo Road

The Waldo house was marvelous. Each couple had a private bedroom, the children shared a bedroom, and the cats had the run of Southern Oregon. Constance decorated our room like a jewel box. She hung the ceiling with a huge colorful poof of an Indian bedspread and color coordinated all our bedding and pillows.

The only thing wrong with our new communal environment was that Constance and I did not get very much privacy. After all, we were newlyweds and still pretty frisky. A week or so after we arrived we declined an invitation to join the others on an overnight visit to the famous Sunny Valley commune and seized the opportunity for some time alone.

While Constance soaked in a hot bath I thought I would sit and meditate near the fire and listen to some music. If it had been six months earlier I would have also lit up a joint, but one of the first things we learned about Oregon was that marijuana and psychedelics were not readily available. For the most part, country hippies got high the old fashioned way—yoga, pranayama, and natural food.

I took off my boots, put on a Beatles album, settled into a half lotus and took some deep breaths. I closed my eyes and used the familiar tracks of the music as a mantra. Everything seemed perfect.

There's nothing you can do that can't be done.[1]

"Wow," I thought, "that is just like something out of the *Tao Te Ching*."

Nothing you can sing that can't be sung.

"Yes, just like the *Tao Te Ching*!"

Nothing you can say but you can learn how to play the game. It's easy.

There was nothing unusual about projecting cosmic significance to popular music, especially that of the Beatles. But that night I was taking it particularly personally.

Nothing you can make that can't be made.
No one you can save that can't be saved.
Nothing you can do but you can learn how to be you in time. It's easy.

The second time I heard the words *"it's easy,"* I felt as if I would burst. I was no longer listening to the stereo. The song had become nothing less than a direct communication from God to my soul. I was so thrilled that I squeezed my buttocks with a contorted shiver of religious ecstasy. Instantly, shivering pangs of intense tingling exploded in my abdomen and between my shoulder blades.

---

[1] *All You Need Is Love.* by John Lennon and Paul McCartney. Copyright © 1967 (Renewed) Sony/ATV Songs LLC. All rights administered by Sony/ATV Music Publishing, 8 Music Square West, Nashville, TN 37203. All rights reserved. Used by permission.

All you need is love.
All you need is love.
All you need is love, love. Love is all you need.

"Oh yes!" The more I surrendered to the tingling, the stronger the tingling, and the more personal the lyrics became.

Nothing you can know that isn't known.
Nothing you can see that isn't shown.
Nowhere you can be that isn't where you're meant to be.
It's easy.

This time when God told me it was "easy" the tingling burst like a balloon at the very top of my head. It was as if an egg of electric fire shattered on my crown and sent scintillating goo slowing dripping over my head.

All you need is love.

"Surrender," I told myself.

All you need is love.

"Surrender. This is it! Let it happen. It won't happen unless you let it."

All you need is love, love. Love is all you need.

Miraculously, I took my own advice. I let go. I surrendered to the tingling at the top of my head, and as I did it became so intense that everywhere it spread it obliterated all sense of separateness. As it covered my head I could no longer see, feel, or conceive of my head as being anything other than everything that was. Wherever the electric fire touched became everywhere, everything. I was becoming universally wall-to-wall from the head down. I could feel my lips, but I could also feel the air that touched my lips, and everything the air that touched my lips touched, and on and on until my lips lost all meaning except to serve as position for the perfect center of the cosmos.

As I continued to surrender it rapidly expanded to the back of my neck and down my spine to usurp the lesser tingling between my shoulder blades. From there it spread to my arms and hands.

All you need is love (All together, now!) All you need is love (Everybody!) All you need is love, love. Love is all you need.

Almost with a thud it reached the base of my spine and flowed into my legs and feet; but then—I had no feet. The *new-I* reached to the innermost/outermost corners of universe, of space and time and energies. The only thing that remained of *old-I* was the part that observes, the part that *realizes*—realizes that it is the *One Big Whatever-it-is*; realizes that its fiery, blissful consciousness fills every nook and cranny of the *One Big Whatever-it is*; realizes that this "thisness" is eternally this!

But *old-I*, the fleshy-fat and blood-filled tumor at the center of the *One Big Whatever-it-is*, also realized that it was losing itself; realized it was dying; realized that its lumbering crust hadn't taken a breath in a long time.

Love is all you need (love is all you need)
Love is all you need (love is all you need)
Love is all you need (love is all you need)
Love is all you need (love is all you need)

The *One Big Whatever-it-is* didn't particularly care that *old-I* might be dying. Things were forever dying and being created in *One Big Whatever-it-is*. It said to itself, "*Old-I* is lucky to die united to the *One Big Whatever-it-is*. Isn't that the spiritual goal of all *old-Is*?"

Old-I was afraid. Maybe it was too soon to say goodbye to *old-I*. It searched the immensity of everywhere to locate an *old-I* hand or an *old-I* foot. Movement might break the spell of reverie the *One Big Whatever-it-is* held upon *old I*. But, fearful as it was, *old-I* loved being one with the *One Big Whatever-it-is* so much that it felt like blasphemy—spiritual suicide—to leave this bliss.

Fear triumphed. An arm moved, and in doing so voluntarily separated itself from the *One Big Whatever-it-is*. The arm lost the omnipresent tingle. Then the other arm moved. Wriggling feet were the next mutinous angels cast from paradise.

I slumped forward and gasped for life, sucking in great waves of stinking air that caused my heart to race like a hummingbird's. The magick fire withdrew from all my extremities and lingered for a few last seconds in the back of my neck. Then it was gone. The stereo was silent. I opened my eyes to discover that a cat had shit on my boots.

CHAPTER 9

Wizard of Takilma

On June 5, 1968, after winning the California Presidential Primary election, Robert F. Kennedy was shot to death in the pantry of the Ambassador Hotel in Los Angeles. The consensus around the hippie campfires was that the evil forces of the proverbial military industrial complex were firmly in charge of the domestic situation. Fearing things would get worse for those with dissident philosophies, many of our neighbors made plans to go even deeper into the woods.

Karl and Elsa liked what they had seen at the Sunny Valley commune and soon moved there with their children and some of the cats. A month or so afterward we saw their smiling faces on the cover of Life Magazine. The photo spread on the inside featured Karl and Elsa as well. Today you can find those same pictures in numerous coffee-table pictorials of the 60s.

The DuQuettes were not so anxious to submit to the hard work and disciplined lifestyle of formal communal life. We pooled our money and bought half an acre of land by the Illinois River near Takilma. Marc and Margaret pitched a tent on the property and set up the home base for our house-building efforts. Constance and I moved nearby in a magical little one-room cabin behind the massive renovated barn that was the home of the Wizard of Takilma Road.

Gary DuBois didn't look like much of a wizard. He was a quiet man about five-and-a-half feet tall and almost skinny. He had a thick black beard that he kept well trimmed. He smiled all the time, and spoke with a charming French-Canadian accent. He lived with his wife, Diane, a huge woman easily three times his size, and their 10-year-old son Andre.

Their home was the envy of everyone on Takilma Road. From the outside it was a huge barn, complete with all the exterior adornments one usually expects to see on an old barn: hubcaps, horseshoes, and an assortment of dear antlers and animal pelts. The centerpiece was the skin of a large brown bear complete with head and claws.

The interior was bizarre to say the least. It was one big room partitioned here and there by antique bookcases, bureaus, secretaries and wardrobes. Two walls were taken up completely, floor to roof (there was no ceiling), with makeshift bookcases crammed full of books. (Gary admitted to having over three thousand, but there could easily have been twice that number.) In the southeast corner near the front door Diane had her kitchen. Illuminated on two walls by large cheery windows, it could have served as the cozy model for a Beatrix Potter story. Her altar was a huge, light green enameled wood stove and warming oven upon which she invoked the most amazing delicacies that she crammed in your mouth each time you entered her world. Gary worked all night at a local dairy, and during the day performed the usual chores around the farmstead. I'm not sure when he slept.

Our little cabin was close enough to the DuBois' barn for us to hear Gary and Diane fighting at night. Actually it was just Diane who did the fighting. Once she started yelling at Gary about one thing or another, he would escape by astrally projecting to safety. He was only successful if he could get to the couch and pop out before Diane saw what was going on (she described herself as being "cursed" with clairvoyance).

One night Constance and I were awakened by the sound of dishes smashing against the barn's wall.

"You're not going to float out of here while I'm talking to you!" The voice was Diane's, and she meant business. Another plate crashed into the wall.

"Get back, dammit, or I'll move your little-assed body where you'll never find it!"

We heard Gary's pitiful mumblings, then another dish hit the wall.

"Okay! Okay! Stop it now. I'm back."

Early the next morning Diane came to our cabin with a plate of cheese blintzes and an explanation of the previous night's events.

"He does it just to irritate me. I can see him do it. I wish I couldn't. If he gets too far away he can stay out for hours. But if I catch him just as he's leaving I can bring the little fart back. Last night I nailed him with a soup bowl. Bam! Right through the skinny little spook."

Gary was a pranic[1] healer—a skill that made him somewhat of a folk hero in Southern Oregon. People from as far away as Grants Pass and Medford traveled to the barn to receive his treatments. Constance and I were privileged to watch him at work on a number of conditions including asthma attacks and broken bones. However, the most amazing thing I ever saw him do was resurrect a dead cat.

---

[1] The ancient Hindus postulated the existence of prana, the vital life force which permeates air, water, sunlight and all living things. They further theorize that the yogi can, by mastering certain techniques of breath control (pranayama), increase this vital force in his or her own body and transmit its healing energy to others.

Like most of our neighbors, the DuBois were slaves to a menagerie of barnyard animals. Diane's favorites were a pair of toy poodles named Shoo-Shoo and Misty. Constance and I were very impressed by the character and intelligence of these critters and when Misty had her next litter (sired by the neighbor's dog Tudypoo) we were the first in line for a pup.[2]

Diane also raised Siamese cats who, it seemed, found a way to breed with every feline in Southern Oregon. Predictably, the yard was alive with kittens that were just too cute for words. One warm summer evening I accidentally stepped on one and crushed the poor thing to death. I was wearing my heavy work boots. It didn't have a chance. I was hurrying to the barn (probably to see what Diane was cooking) and came down full force on the tiny fur-ball. I heard it crunch with several sickening cracks that told me it was mortally injured. I dropped to my knees to see its last pitiful struggles. I had obviously broken its spine. Its back legs were completely motionless and just for a moment it waved its front paws in the air. It was so little. The last breath inflated its wee body like a tiny balloon and then exited through the bloody mouth and nose, creating shiny red bubbles that quivered for an instant before popping in the warm evening air.

I was so upset that I couldn't think straight. I even considered going back to our cabin and not telling anyone what happened. "Diane is going to kill me," I thought. I decided that I would have to face the music sooner or later. After all, how can you lie to a psychic? I picked up the little carcass. It fit easily in the palm of my hand. The black eyes were wide open and its mouth agape. I knocked at the door. Diane opened it and immediately saw everything.

"Oh you big oaf! Bring it in! Bring it in!"

---

[2] This little sweetie we named Shep, and he remained our faithful companion until his death fourteen years later.

She snatched her dead kitten by the scruff of its neck and held it up to show Gary. Its crooked body swung from her hand like a wet rag.

"Look what Sleeping Bear[3] did, stomping around the barnyard in the dark!"

I babbled a score of groveling apologies.

Gary was seated on the couch in a full lotus posture smiling from ear to ear, wearing nothing but black Speedos.

"Bring it here. Bring it here," he said with a twinkle in his eye that I mistook for a tear.

"Gary, I'm sorry. It's dead. I broke its back. I crunched it with my full weight. I'm really sorry."

"We'll see," he said as Diane put the kitten in his hand.

"Oh God!" I thought. "He's going to try to bring it back to life."

"It might be the wrong time," Gary giggled as he began to go to work.

He held the kitten in the palm of his left hand and used his right hand to trace rings and spheres in the air around the body. His gestures and movements were intensely graceful, and as I watched him I could almost see colored lines of energy radiating from his palm and fingertips, wrapping the kitten in what looked like a vibrating ball of twine.

After ten minutes or so of making spherical motions, he held his hand over various parts of the kitten's body and took a series of deep breaths that he held for an impressively long time. Alternately, he emptied his lungs and held his negative breath for equally long periods. The whole atmosphere in the room became charged. My own hands and fingers tingled as I watched Gary work. Diane sat in the kitchen with her eyes closed.

---

[3] Diane gave everybody "Indian" names (usually to ridicule physical abnormalities or character flaws.) I was dubbed "Sleeping Bear" because of my girth and laziness. She named Constance "Smiling Squirrel" because—well, have you ever seen a picture of Constance?

I was very impressed by what was obviously a psychic tour-de-force, but it still didn't alter the fact that the kitten was dead—really dead, and all these heroics were not going to change that. I was more than a little embarrassed for Gary. He was trying so hard to be the neighborhood holy man. This was the first time I had ever seen him fail at a spiritual chore. I felt extra guilty about the whole thing.

He began to violently stroke the air on four sides of the kitten, creating, as it were, a pyramidal field. With each stroke he raised his left hand almost as if he were going to toss the kitten in the air. If it were alive, I thought, it would sure be getting a thrill out of that. All these rough movements jostled the little body back and forth giving the appearance of animation.

I watched Gary for nearly a half an hour and was anxious to go home and put this sad evening behind me. I looked over at Diane, hoping to get some encouragement to leave, but her eyes were still tightly shut. Gary began the entire cycle of techniques over again; first the sphere, then the breathing, then the tossing. He repeated the cycle, this time faster, then again, and again, until finally his left hand dropped to his lap and I heard what sounded like a kitten's cough. Gary wiped a plug of brown blood from his naked leg. The kitten rolled back and forth in Gary's hand and coughed again. He turned his tiny patient on its back and began to "work" on its underbelly. Immediately more brown liquid came out its mouth. I moved closer to see. It was alive. There was no doubt about it. It was alive.

Gary picked it up by the scruff of its neck and tried to get it to sit up in his hand. Its forelegs seemed willing but it had no control of its hindquarters.

"You're right." Gary giggled. They were the first words he had spoken since beginning the treatment. "You broke his spine."

"Big oaf!" Diane chimed in without opening her eyes.

Gary went to work on the back. Using the thumb and fore-finger of his right hand he rolled and twisted the air like he was rolling an invisible cigarette. He started between the kitten's ears and moved slowly down to the tip of its tail. He reminded me of a child playing doctor on a pretend patient, but it was more than pretending. As I watched his fingers move I could clearly see what he was visualizing. I looked over at Diane. Her eyes were still closed but I knew she, too, shared in the vision. Gary was braiding the spine in his imagination, and Diane and I were helping. For a few golden moments I saw how everything in the universe is alive and connected to everything else. Everything is alive and nothing is impossible if you can visualize it perfectly enough.

Within a few minutes the kitten's back legs were thrashing wildly and Gary was having difficulty keeping the little critter in his hand. Before I went home, I watched the dead kitten sit up on the coffee table, scratch its ear with its hind leg and yawn. In the morning it was out in the barnyard wrestling with its brothers and sisters. Diane named it Lazarus.

Later that week, Gary accidentally backed over Lazarus with the pickup truck. I watched him dig its shallow grave behind the chicken coop.

"I guess now's the right time," he giggled.

CHAPTER 10

Rock-n-Roll Rosicrucian

The time we spent in Oregon was the golden age of hippiedom. We were surrounded by hard-core spiritual seekers, yogis, Buddhists, and devotional Christians. God was the centerpiece of every conversation, every meal, every diversion and pleasure. We were like an Amish community—only with a perverse sense of humor, a love of music and bright colors, and raging libidos.

With expert help from our talented hippie neighbors we completed Marc and Margaret's house in early September, and laid out plans to build another for Constance and me. As we were nearly out of money, we decided to return briefly to Southern California and raise the needed funds. I was sure I would be able to find work singing, and if all went well, we would be back in Oregon in two or three weeks.

As it turned out, things went extremely well. The first day back I joined my old song writing partner Charley Harris, who had secured a marvelous gig at one of the better Newport Beach

Charlie D. & Milo, Epic Records, 1970

eateries. He negotiated more money from the club and gener-
ously allowed me to share the stage.

Charley and I were pretty good. The fact that we wrote
many of the songs we performed made our cabaret act somewhat of an aberration. We sang five nights a week and by the
end of the second week I had earned the fabled grubstake. We

packed up the old VW bus and readied ourselves for our tri-
umphant return to Oregon. We planned to depart immediately after my last Saturday night performance. As it turned
out, we did not leave that night, nor would we ever return to
our land.

It happened that Charley and I had an old drinking buddy
who had recently "bought into" the music business. He
chanced to teamed up with a seasoned producer from Co-
lumbia Records, and together they shepherded their client to
two number one hits in less than ninety days. Their stock in
the industry was at its zenith and for some reason they chose
that night to get drunk and listen to Charley and me. They
liked our original songs and asked us if we had written any
others. Charley lied and boasted that we had *hundreds* of ·
songs. Hearing this, they asked if we would be willing to record
a demo. Neither Charley nor I actually thought this was anything other than Hollywood hype, but I agreed to stay another week to see if they would deliver.

They delivered—and more. Two days later we drove to Sunset Boulevard and recorded a few original songs in historic Studio A at CBS. Within the week we signed to record two singles
and an album on the Epic label,[1] joined the obligatory unions,
and signed with the William Morris Agency. It was an adolescent's
dream come true. Charley and I and everyone who knew us were
stunned. It was now our turn to deliver all those songs we said
we had written.

---

[1] We called ourselves Charley D. & Milo. Our first single on the Epic label
was *"Back Bay Blu."* Our album, simply called Charley D. & Milo, did
remarkably well everywhere it was distributed. It even earned Billboard
Magazine's spotlight pick and received good reviews. Our second single,
"The Word is Love" went to number one in the handful of cities where dis-
tribution enabled it to be broadcast and purchased. Salt Lake City was one
such city, and the highlight of our concert visit to that fair city was hearing it played on two AM stations simultaneously.

Realizing we were philosophical light-weights with very little to say, we nonetheless chose to take the high road and channel the themes for our songs by flipping through the pages of an occult dictionary and picking a word or phrase at random. We wrote of sylphs and gnomes and undines and white goose feet. We thought it was all very "heavy."[2] Even our publisher got caught up in our magick music and renamed his company "Hazelwand Publishing."

For the next four years Charley and I played (sometimes quite successfully) at being recording artists and musicians. We traveled everywhere our songs received radio play and were the opening act for more recognizable names. A few of our songs were picked up and recorded by other groups and we garnered more than our share of collateral studio work.[3]

Predictably, Charley and I fell prey to the excesses that accompanied such lifestyles in the early 70s, and it became more and more obvious that I was soon going to have to make a decision about my future as a holy man. In spite of the craziness, Constance and I decided we wanted a baby. Our son, Jean-Paul, was born toward the end of this wild and unhealthy season of my life. His arrival made it clear that the unstable world of a hippie musician was not conducive to family life. I decided to get out of the business and take my chances in the real world. For the next ten years or so I didn't do a very good job of it.

---

[2] "My own eye me mirror be. Neophyte he turn the key. Paradoxically I weep to laugh." (Theme from Mt. Oread.)

[3] 60s recording star Johnny Rivers saw us performing at Hollywood's Troubadour and liked our song "*Moving to the Country*" so much that he recorded it on his next album "*Home Grown.*" Charley and I and our lead guitarist joined him on the session. About that same time I really "went Hollywood" after I was accidentally accepted at the Lee Strasberg Theatrical Institute. For over a year I was inexplicably privileged to study with that great master and his team of unforgettable character actors.

While trying to figure out what I wanted to do when I grew up, my brother Marc encouraged me to join him in the Rosicrucian Order AMORC. He said they were like mystic Freemasons. I took his advice, and with the United States Postal Service as my psychopomp, I took the first initiatory step into the Western Mysteries. My employment and financial difficulties would not get better for a long time, but my spiritual life was about to explode.

CHAPTER 11

My Father's Ghost

Most everyone would agree that objective reality is a world where living things are just that—living things, such as people, or dogs, or cats, or elephants. Furthermore, symbols are not alive, but are abstract representations of ideas.

It has been my experience, however, that the opposite is true on the magical plane. Symbols are alive and living things are generally symbols of something. When I see an angel or a magical beast in a dream or vision or skrying[1] session, it is usually a symbolic encounter with a concept concerning a personal or magical issue that is too complex to be expressed or understood through any other medium.

---

[1] Skrying (scrying), sometimes called "traveling in the spirit vision," is a name given to a variety of clairvoyant experiences usually induced by formal magical procedures. One can skry a material object to psychically *see* the spiritual reality underlying its existence or learn of its magical past. Also, in magical systems, such as the Enochian magick of Dr. John Dee, one can converse with spirits or visit their environment via visions seen in crystals or mirrors or which simply appear in the "mind's eye."

These same "living" apparitions react to symbols as if they were alive. A simple geometric figure such as a cross or a pentagram drawn in the air in the face of a pesky spirit is often enough to send it fleeing in terror. This basic rule of thumb unravels when one is faced in dream or vision with the living image of a dead person. Is it alive, or is it a symbol?

Almost everyone who has ever lost a loved one has at least one visitation story to tell. Usually the deceased appears in a vivid dream or vision a week or two after dying and delivers a message to the effect that everything is okay and not to worry. I used to think that this phenomenon was a natural denial mechanism of the mind, triggered at times when it is easier to accept an hallucination rather than dealing with grief and the great mystery of death. Now, I am not so sure.

I was 24 when my father died of emphysema a few weeks after seeing Jean-Paul take his first steps. He was only 61. About ten days after his funeral he showed up to deliver a curious message.

Since my initiation into AMORC I had set aside an hour or two each Thursday night to study the monographs and practice the various outlined "psychic" exercises. For some reason I decided this night I would perform my devotions before dinner and set up my Sanctum altar in the bedroom.

I opened the "temple" with the usual ceremonial formalities, unsealed my new monograph and started to read. Almost immediately I found that I could not keep my mind focused on the words. I found myself reading the same sentence over and over again until I became extremely sleepy. I finally gave up trying to read altogether and decided to take a little nap before dinner and pick up my studies later. I blew out both candles and stretched out in the cool darkness. In those days it was my habit, when sleeping on my back, to cross my arms over my breast. I closed my eyes and was instantly out.

Suddenly I became conscious that the room was no longer dark. I remember thinking that I had broken the very first safety rule of fledgling mystics and allowed myself to fall asleep with candles burning. I opened my eyes and looked up at the ceiling. I could see every detail bathed in a warm orange light. Then I noticed that my arms were no longer crossed over my chest but stretched out crucifixion style. That struck me as being very curious because I knew I hadn't been asleep long enough to change positions.

The pit of my stomach tingled with the joyous thrill I always feel when I dream of flying. But I wasn't flying. I was flat on my back on the bed. I turned my head to the left and looked down my arm to see my hand dangling over the mattress. Then I turned to the right and to my utter delight discovered my father sitting by the bed not six inches from my right hand.

He looked great, better, in fact, than I had seen him in years. I felt younger just looking at him. His skin was a beautiful tan and his hair was thicker and darker than I ever remembered. He didn't say a word, and for some reason I wasn't inclined to speak either. We just looked at each other.

I soon became conscious of the peculiarity of the moment. The light in the room did not come from the candles or the electric lights, but seemed to radiate from every object in the room, most especially from Dad and me. Also, there was a tangible silence in the room as if the whole world was holding its breath. I had the feeling that if anything were to move it would do so in blissfully slow motion. Finally, it dawned on me: I was sleeping; Dad was dead; and all this was very weird indeed.

I had the presence of mind to realize that the thrill in the pit of my stomach was symptomatic of astral projection, and this whole experience might not be a dream at all but a bona fide case of psychic contact with the dead. To test my theory I willed myself to float slowly to the ceiling and back down again. I did it with ease. I looked over at Dad and smiled. He seemed amused but a little impatient.

Then, with great deliberation, he lifted his right hand. He wore a beautiful golden ring with a blue stone setting. The stone was embellished with the Masonic square and compass. However, upon closer examination, I saw that superimposed upon the square was a downward pointing triangle surmounted by an ankh, very similar to an AMORC device.

"Is this your message?" I asked mentally.

He smiled and pointed to the ring.

I had no idea what this meant. He delivered the wordless message with such drama and grace that for the time being I didn't care what it meant. It was a just a beautifully pleasant moment. I choked up a little like I do when I almost cry at the movies. I closed my eyes just for an instant to control the tears. I took a deep breath, then opened my eyes. The room was dark. My arms were folded over my chest. My father was gone.

A week or so later Constance and I visited Aunt Vina, my father's sister, in Long Beach. I mentioned to her that I was studying the AMORC monographs and she said, "In that case I've got something for you."

She went to her bookcase and plucked several very old AMORC books and some bound monographs from the 1930s.

"I took the lessons for about five years," she said, as she handed me the books, "You're welcome to these old monographs, too. Your father tried to join when he was 17 or 18, but in those days you had to be 21 years old to join the Rosicrucians. He was heartbroken. He was so thrilled when the Masons accepted him about the time you we born."

This little tidbit of family history did not exactly explain my father's visitation, but at the time it served to encourage me concerning the direction my spiritual life was heading. However, in the years to follow, when the mysteries of Rosicrucianism and esoteric Freemasonry would become the centerpiece of my magical life, I would come to understand that the message of my father's ghost was uncannily prophetic.

CHAPTER 12

Initiation

Hopefully you now have a pretty good idea what raw material the gods had to work with when 24-year-old Lon DuQuette first knocked at the door of the Western Mysteries and demanded admittance. When the door opened I started all over again. I stepped into a world where *effect* sometimes precedes *cause*; a world of living images and symbols whose meanings change profoundly the moment they are defined; a world where saviors can be your worst enemies and demons your only salvation; a nonlinear world where unrelated experiences separated by many years can be impressed simultaneously upon one golden moment of growth or realization.

So it is here that I beg the reader's indulgence, for I must by necessity soon depart from the strict linear chronology of events that has characterized my narrative to this point. Of course I will try to tell things more or less in order, but the importance for doing so will become less and less relevant. I believe it will, however, be helpful to know the following:

I became an enthusiastic student of the Rosicrucian Order AMORC's study program. I joined a local lodge and for several years was very active, serving first as Neophyte class master, then as ritual officer in degree initiations and at weekly convocations. I was especially attracted to the rich symbolism of the degrees. I couldn't get enough of temple work and found that my entire life and dream patterns became refocused and reorganized in harmony with the symbols and symmetry of ritual.

I owe a great debt to AMORC, and I mean no disrespect to this great organization when I say I soon became impatient with the pace of the program.[1] At the invitation of some friends I joined the Traditional Martinist Order and got my first taste of real ceremonial magick, and I also joined the Builders of the Adytum and began studying their marvelous Tarot and Qabalah correspondence courses. I resonated perfectly to this stuff and I was a passionate student.

Eventually I came upon an early edition of Aleister Crowley's Thoth Tarot deck. I had never seen anything so beautiful in my life. The name Aleister Crowley sounded familiar and I vaguely recalled seeing his name footnoted in a Qabalah book by Frater Achad.[2] I referred to my occult dictionary and discovered to my horror—"Aleister Crowley—famous Scottish Satanist..."

---

[1] I confess that I also grew weary of the level of psychic self-righteousness that seemed to infect many of my fellow lodge members. It never fails to amaze me how a self-declared psychic "master" can prattle in my face for half an hour about his or her mind-reading prowess and never have a clue that I am thinking (very loudly) that he or she is the biggest horse's ass in the world. One afternoon at convocation I tested the clairvoyance of one group of self-proclaimed aura voyeurs. During the period of silent meditation I projected into the forbidden "Sanctum" area of the temple and astrally *mooned* the entire assembly. Nobody seemed to notice.

[2] *Q.B.L. or The Bride's Reception,* by Frater Achad. Most recent edition (Kila, MT: Kessinger Publishing Company, L.L.C., 1992).

O.T.O. Caliph Hymenaeus Alpha, IX° 777 (Grady L. McMurtry),
Constance DuQuette, Jean-Paul DuQuette, and the Author, 1978.

I may have been a wild a crazy heretic but I sure didn't want
anything to do with Satanism. Knowing my brother had *The Book
of Thoth* (the deck's companion text), I promptly gave the cards
to him—good riddance!

I was sternly enlightened a few days later by our dear
friend Mad Bob (a name that only begins to describe his bizarre and wonderful character) who had returned briefly from
a Central American adventure. Bob had read Crowley's autobiography[3] and insisted that I would love the man if I gave
him a chance. When I showed him what the occult dictionary
had to say he brushed it off saying, "It doesn't matter if

---

[3] *The Confessions of Aleister Crowley* (London: Penguin/Arkana, 1989).

Crowley was a Satanist, he was a good kind of Satanist and you'll just love him! Trust me."

That was the strangest thing I had ever heard, but I respected Mad Bob's opinion and took the cards back from Marc and asked to borrow *The Book of Thoth.* Bob was right. Even though I didn't understand most of what I read, I knew that Aleister Crowley was brilliant, funny, and everything I was looking for. I bought everything I could by or concerning the man (precious little in those days) and eventually wrote to Crowley's Ordo Templi Orientis (O.T.O.) at the address published on the Caliph card of the Thoth Deck to ask for initiation.

On November 15, 1975 I was initiated in the Minerval Degree (0°) in the O.T.O. by Major Grady McMurtry (Caliph Hymenaeus Alpha, IX°) and Phyllis Seckler (Soror Meral, IX°) at their home in Dublin, California. Constance was initiated about six months later. We had no idea at the time, but the Order was almost extinct. When we were initiated there was only a handful of members still living. Soon after joining the O.T.O. I discontinued my work in AMORC, TMO and BOTA. Once I tasted Crowley nothing else seemed to satisfy.

The O.T.O. is an initiatory order similar to freemasonry. It doesn't provide educational monographs or standardized tests. Rather, it offers members the opportunity to experience a series of dramatic and magical initiations artfully designed to awaken and unfold the candidates' spiritual potentialities. If a member did nothing else with the O.T.O. career but undergo these degree experiences, they would be immeasurably rewarded. Serious members know, however, that there is much more to the O.T.O.'s magick than a two-hour ceremony performed once or twice a year. So profound are the Order's inner mysteries that to penetrate them requires not only a rich magical and spiritual education, but also a high level of meditative attainment. Members who wish to truly affiliate at this level are expected to seize responsibility for their own magical education and eventually rend the veil of the Order's mysteries for themselves.

Initiation is a personal matter. What could be more personal than the evolution of your own soul? One's true initiatory grade has nothing to do with organizations, titles, or degrees. The only degree that counts is the degree to which your soul has evolved. The only degree work possible is learning what needs to be done to take the next step.

I will forever be grateful to the organizations and people who guided me in my studies prior to my entrance to the O.T.O.; but it is the O.T.O. and the magical writings of Aleister Crowley that I must credit for whatever initiatory progress (real or imagined) I have made in this life. In order to make this magick work I have had to train and educate myself in a score of fields not directly connected with magick. I have had to integrate bizarre and abstract spiritual concepts into a daily life of work and marriage and fatherhood and amusement. Everything that follows in this little book must be projected against the backdrop of my life in the O.T.O. (the details of which I hope someday chronicle). For our purposes here I will only summarize as follows:

In 1978 I was chartered by Hymeneus Alpha to form a Lodge of O.T.O. in Newport Beach, CA. Constance and I proceeded to initiate. We were the first local lodge so chartered by the Grand Lodge. Today the Order has approximately three thousand members in forty countries. I have had the privilege to initiate hundreds of individuals around the world and am currently a governing officer in the International Order and United States Deputy Grand Master General.

Sounds pretty impressive, eh? I assure you my magical life has not always been so glamorous.

CHAPTER 13

Nedura and the Procession of Elves

When I was 11, I was quite impressed with an odd little Disney film called "Darby O'Gill and the Little People."[1] It's the tale of a crusty old storyteller, prone to taking a nip or two (played marvelously by Albert Sharpe), who manages to capture the King of the Leprechauns. In exchange for his freedom the king grants him three wishes, all of which, naturally, backfire. It's a cute story designed to delight 11-year-olds, but it struck a deep chord in me.

Somehow, even though I was cynical about God and Jesus, I found it easy to believe that there might be some truth behind legions of elves and fairies and leprechauns. If they existed I wanted to see them. I even tried to induce an altered state of consciousness by exhausting myself on my bicycle in the secluded wilds of Pawnee Park. I never saw anything stranger than mosquitoes.

---

[1] "Darbey O'Gill and The Little People" (1959), Disney Buena Vista. Director: Robert Stevenson.

Still, I might have been on the right track. It has been my experience that most of my significant mystical adventures are triggered by trauma. Perhaps this is true only for the most base and unevolved individuals, those who need to be beaten over the head before they loosen up. It is certainly true for me. Very early in my magical career, following a trauma of sorts, I had a very vivid encounter with a most curious creature.

The nine-month period prior to my initiation into the O.T.O. was perhaps the most traumatic time of my life. We were painfully poor and my prospects, as usual, were dismal. My occult studies were a welcome escape and I used them precisely for that purpose. I was especially passionate about my BOTA tarot lessons and was about to begin painting the twenty-two cards of the major arcana.

One afternoon Constance and I took the baby and drove to the market to buy whatever we could with the fifteen dollars I had just earned from giving guitar lessons. Constance, as usual, was a wise and frugal shopper and managed to spend less than ten dollars. Using a coupon, she even bought us a special treat of half a pound of freshly ground Ethiopian Harrar coffee (my last remaining drug of choice). I couldn't wait to get home, get wired and paint my first tarot card.

Unfortunately, when we arrived home we discovered that, in the confusion of putting the baby in the car, we left our bag of precious groceries in the shopping cart. I got in the car and sped back to the store. It was too late. Our groceries were gone. I was furious. I was sick. I was crazy.

I went back in the store and with our last five dollars bought the baby's vegetables and (in an act of obscene selfishness) another half pound of Ethiopian Harrar. I was so upset that I could hardly drive. It was probably a good thing that I ran out of gas about six blocks from home. With no money for gas, I abandoned the car and walked home. I handed Constance the baby's vegetables and without a word headed straight for the espresso machine. I packed it tightly full of that incredible coffee and stared at it until the mad hissing stopped. I poured myself a triple shot and locked myself in the bedroom with my paints and tarot cards.

I finished the card in about two hours. It was beautiful. After slugging down another triple espresso, I set my beautiful Fool up on my little altar and stared at it until bedtime. Even though I was wired to the gills I was very sleepy. I apologized to Constance for my crabbiness and fell instantly asleep.

A chain of meaningless unrelated dreams eventually put me behind the wheel of my car. I had to get it home. I had never abandoned it before. It wouldn't start. Of course! It was out of gas. I got out of the car to do god knows what, and bumped into what I can only describe as a leprechaun. He was about eight inches high and wore a black suit and a top hat that had been crushed to a comic angle. I sat down in the street to get a better look. He had lamb chop sideburns and a nose like W. C. Fields. He produced a giant-sized (giant-sized for him) silver flask and unscrewed the top.

"I made it m'self," he said as he offered it to me. "One for the road. Drink it all. You've never had anythin' like it. I made it m'self."

I took the flask and drained it. It had the smell and taste of fine whiskey but without any of the bite or burn. I became instantly drunk and was getting drunker by the second. The little man disappeared. I got back in the car and started it. I put the automatic gearshift to "Drive" only to find myself moving backwards. I put it in "Reverse" and the whole car slid violently to the right. Finally, I somehow got it going straight ahead but when I turned the steering wheel to the right the car moved left and visa versa. I didn't know what to do. I slammed on the brakes, which made me go faster. Eventually I crashed through a chain link fence and drove the car straight into a swimming pool.

I opened the door and stepped out of the car and into the shallow pool. I was naked and covered in what looked like soapsuds. I was no longer drunk. I felt clean and holy as if I had just been baptized. I waded to the shallow end of the pool and stepped out of the water. The sun was setting and it colored the sky with a most brilliant array of pastel colors. Everything in the vision was pastel. I saw no primary colors. A road skirted the swimming pool. It snaked to the horizon in wide, lazy S's until it narrowed in exaggerated perspective and disappeared completely into the setting sun.

I was witnessing a parade—a disorganized procession of the most exotic and whimsical creatures I had ever seen or imagined. No two were alike. They were humanoid. Most were tall and slender, but each wore a different style and pastel color costume and hat. Each one was very attractive but was impossible to determine if they were male or female.

The most amazing thing about them was their transparency. I could see through their clothes and I could see through them. I thought to myself, "these are elves or fairies." The creatures reacted to my thought with riotous approval and began playing gaily upon bizarre musical instruments. There were thousands of them stretching all the way to the sun. As they marched past me, they waved and blew kisses to me. I was absolutely delighted and enchanted.

Eventually one of the "elves" broke rank and approached me. This one, I concluded, was female because she was the most delicately beautiful creature I had ever seen. She was very thin and wore sheaths of transparent lavender that alternately clung tightly to her firm little body then streamed lightly in the air around her. Her skin was light mauve and her hair transparent pink— bobbed in a classic pixie cut. She smiled at me as I recognized her as a mystical friend from a thousand unremembered dreams.

She carried in her hands an octagonal paper box with thousands of little pink wheels printed on the sides. The wheels had spokes like the wheels that adorn the Fool's jacket on the 0 Key of the Tarot.

I wanted to tell her how happy I was to see her and ask her how we could meet again. Before I could phrase the words, she handed me the box and removed the lid.

"Whenever you want to be with me, you need only look into the box and say..."

Suddenly from nowhere a cosmic organist played an arpeggio. Taking it as her queue she sang the following song to the tune of "Silver bells, Silver bells, it's Christmas time in the city."

"Nedura, Nedura, play by myself—in the rain."

It seemed perfectly logical to me at the time. I looked into the box. It was filled a quarter full with fine light lavender powder. As I repeated the words, "Nedura, Nedura, play by myself— in the rain," my breath kicked up the powder and created great clouds of lavender dust that obscured the whole vision.

I didn't know what any of this meant, but I suddenly became aware that I was experiencing a vision. I knew that if I could wake myself up fast enough I would be able to write it all down before I forgot it. I didn't want to lose Nedura again.

As I fought to regain consciousness I looked at the little wheels on the box. They were all turning. The whole field of my vision was filled with turning wheels. I opened my eyes and still saw them turning on the walls and ceiling of my bedroom. I reached over and turned on the lamp. I could see everything in the room clearly, but I also continued to see thousands of turning wheels superimposed upon everything. I grabbed a pencil and an envelope I was using as a bookmark and quickly wrote down everything I could remember. Eventually the wheels disappeared from my vision. Before I went back to sleep I got up and turned the Fool card face down on the altar.

Nedura never visited me again.[2] For years I tried in vain to invoke and evoke her by chanting her crazy little song while visualizing that octagonal box. I've investigated her name using the Hebrew and Greek Qabalah and failed to find anything of significance. I even tried to conjure her into a Solomonic triangle and summon her through rites of which I am forbidden to speak—all to no avail. She remains a mystery.

---

[2] At least as far as I remember.

CHAPTER 14

My Magick Wand

My Minerval initiation into the O.T.O. marked the beginning of my formal magical life. Even though the Order is not obliged to function as a teaching vehicle, my initiators suggested that I begin the programs of study and practice that Crowley outlined in *One Star in Sight*[1] and various other texts. This work included preliminary yogic exercises, both physical and meditative, and the beginning rituals of ceremonial magick. I embraced the work with great energy and passion. Today, twenty-three years later, when I look at my magical journals of that period, I am exhausted just reading about my routine.

I rose before dawn; performed the banishing rituals of the pentagram and hexagram. I then limbered up with yoga, eleven rounds of an eleven-fold solar adoration, after which I settled

---

[1] *Magick - Book Four - Liber ABA - Appendix II.* by Aleister Crowley (York Beach, ME: Samuel Weiser, 1997), p. 486.

APRIL 5   [DOUZG]

UP 5:45am 207lbs

FASTING - 12 hrs so far
YOGA 4 cycles - Neck still prohibitive
Good ploosh -
HIGH CLOUDS Come on patio -

PRANAYAMA - 1hour & 16 MIN WOW!, Thur
I will change pranayama cycle on ~~xxxxx~~
4:00pm - FASTING 24hrs - Continued
Just returned from Come walk

11:30pm   OPUS NEUF - IMAGE STRONG - ELIXIR
very well mixed. sweet - Annointed Sigit HOST.
MY-BODY (H.M.B FIRST) Sigil then removed from
△ - To covered altar - I'm leaving the circle
UP AND THE △ IN place.
Feeling of Relief & optimism

Figure 1.   Diary Madness. Pages from Author's diary.

into my asana[2] and did pranayama.[3] I concluded the meditation period with exercises designed to increase my concentration skills, then closed with a repeat of the banishing rituals of the pentagram and hexagram.

I was faithful to my regimen. As the months progressed I increased the times and levels of difficulty of my pranayama and meditation exercises,[4] and replaced the banishing rituals with Crowley's more advanced Thelemic rituals.

I should like to point out that my notes from this period indicate that I did not have a clue *why* I was doing all these things. Still, I ploughed on and looked anxiously forward to my next O.T.O. initiation. When it came I felt that I was ready to cut my magick wand.

The magician is armed with four fundamental weapons: the wand, the cup, the sword and the disk. These four weapons are symbolic of the powers of the great qabalistic four-letter deity Yod-Heh-Vav-Heh. The four letters in the name are, in turn, symbolic of the four qabalistic worlds: Atziluth, the Archetypal world; Briah, the Creative world; Yetzirah, the Formative world; and Assiah, the Material world. These four worlds have their counterparts in the human soul; Chiah, the life force; Neschamah, the divine soul-intuition; Ruach, the intellect; and Nephesh, the animal soul.[5]

---

[2] My asana at that time was the Dragon, a classic Japanese posture, kneeling with the knees and legs together and the buttocks resting on the heels of the feet.

[3] The ancient Hindus postulated the existence of prana, the vital life force which permeates air, water, sunlight and all living things. They further theorize that the yogi can, by mastering certain techniques of breath control (pranayama), increase this vital force in his or her own body and transmit its healing energy to others.

[4] Yes, I could sit for an ungodly length of time with a teacup filled to the brim balanced on my head without spilling a drop. It is an ability for which I have yet to find a need.

[5] See chapter 15, Evocation of Orobas.

Table 1.   *Attributes and Weapons of the Great Name.*

Great Name	י Yod	ה Heh	ו Vav	ה Heh
Qabalistic World	Atziluth Archetypal	Briah Creative	Yetzirah Formative	Assiah Material
Parts of the Soul	Chiah Life Force	Neschamah, Divine soul-intuition	Ruach Intellect	Nephesh Animal Soul
Elements	Fire	Water	Air	Earth
Elemental Beings	Salamanders	Undines	Sylphs	Gnomes
Magical Weapons	Wand (Will)	Cup (Understanding -Heart)	Sword (Mind -Intellect)	Disk (Emotions -Body)

Finally, all of these four-part concepts can be expressed meta-phorically as the four fundamental elements of Fire, Water, Air and Earth. See Table 1, above.

The disk is the first weapon to be constructed, for it is the foundation of the magician's career. The disk is also called the *pan*tacle because it should display, in symbolic language, the to-tality of the magician's magical worldview—the magician's uni-verse. Upon this universe, the magician applies the discriminat-ing power of intellect (the sword) in order to learn the mysteries of God and self (Knowledge is Power). To truly understand this power and wield it wisely, the magician must learn to listen to the counsel of the heart (cup). Finally, the magician earns the wand by realization of his or her true purpose. The wand is the Will and the Will is the supreme weapon of the magician.

Even though the wand is the last weapon a magician should make, it was the first one that I wanted. The thought of tracing my pentagrams and hexagrams with a real wand and brandishing it against pesky spirits and demons was just too powerful an image for my poor ego to resist. I had to have that wand.

Magical literature abounds with traditions concerning how the magician goes about creating magical weapons. The wand should be of almond wood[6] cut from a flowering tree on the day of Corpus Christi. It should be cut with one blow from a magick knife (which the magician must also make), and it should be the length of the space between the tip of the fingers and the elbow. One end of the wand should be identified somehow with the male principle and one end female. Once it is straightened and dried it must be peeled and smoothed, then wrapped in a black cloth[7] until it is consecrated with an elaborate ceremony. After that it is to be kept in the altar, wrapped in a scarlet bag.

That's what I wanted. The only thing standing between me and magical adeptship was not having that wand!

---

[6] The three Paths of the middle pillar of the Tree of Life (the most balanced and direct path from material existence to supreme godhead—of which the human spine is the microcosmic reflection) are נ, ס, and ת. These three letters enumerate to 463. Moses' brother-in-law, Aaron, was in charge of a mighty rod of power made of the wood of an almond tree. This is the same rod that performed all manner of wonders before Pharaoh's magicians. The Hebrew words for "a rod of almond" (מטה השקד) also enumerates to the prime 463, making the almond rod the ultimate wand of power.

[7] An unconsecrated magical weapon is like a uninitiated candidate for initiation. At the beginning of the ceremony the candidate is hoodwinked. So too, before the consecration of the weapon it is kept in darkness until the magician brings it to light.

My First Degree initiation had been scheduled. I knew there were two lovely almond trees in the backyard garden of my initiator's home. I was sure that if I asked nicely I could cut my wand there. In the meantime I wanted to have a practice wand, so I joined a few crazy friends on a midnight raid on a backyard in Huntington Beach known to have an almond tree. It was great fun. We felt so evil. My naughty stolen practice wand looked pretty good.

Finally the day of my First Degree arrived and I traveled again to Dublin to be initiated. First Degree in the O.T.O. is symbolic of birth, and I could not think of a more auspicious day to cut my magick wand. I was granted permission to take it from one of the trees in the garden. I took my time and carefully scanned the trees from top to bottom. I spotted the perfect candidate, a very straight section about twenty inches in length. It was budding and ready to flower. About ten inches of it were very dark, as if the branch grew during a cold or difficult season. Then the wood turned very light in color all the way to the end. This light and dark feature was most attractive because it fulfilled traditional male/female requirements.

The branch was very high in the tree and to my frustration there was no ladder at hand tall enough to reach it. Grady suggested that if I stood on the very top of the ladder and used the long pruning sheers I could do it. He offered to stand on the ladder below me and support me by holding on to my belt buckle. I was scared to death but I gave it a try. I can still remember looking down at Grady, his hand clutching the waistband of my pants, Aleister Crowley's golden seal ring flashing from his finger in the sunlight.

I severed the branch with one blow and my prize tumbled to the garden floor. Grady helped me down and we laughed like schoolboys. This was going to be the best magical wand in the world!

Once back home I constructed a fixture out of a board and a few nails and put my precious wand in the straightening device. It took nearly three months to dry and straighten to my liking. In the meantime I used my stolen substitute wand in all my daily rituals.

Finally the wand was ready to remove from the fixture. I trimmed it and sanded it to a sensuous smoothness. I oiled it with olive oil and rubbed to a perfect polish. I can't tell you how beautiful it was. It was dark brown to the middle then it turned a brilliant creamy light green. I sewed a red satin bag where it would live after its consecration. Until then, I stored it wrapped in a black cloth.

Nothing would be too good for my wand. I composed a fourteen-day ceremony of consecration that would begin on the evening of the new moon and climax on the full moon in Aries (cardinal fire). I constructed the ceremony around the Preliminary Invocation of the Goetia[8] and it's barbarous words of evocation.

Each night after banishing and opening my living room temple, I removed the wand from its black wrapping and set it before a bowl of flaming alcohol in the East.[9] I then recited the Preliminary Invocation and performed the Greater Invoking Ritual of the Pentagram Fire, after which I passed the wand through the flames, reciting the barbarous words of evocation to call forth the spirits of Fire. I then returned the wand to its black wrapping and banished and closed the temple.

On the second night I repeated the ceremony as before, but I recited *two* rounds of the barbarous words, the third night three rounds, etc., until by the last night I found myself whipped up into quite a frenzy by fourteen rounds of the barbarous words of

---

[8] See *The Magick of Thelema* by Lon Milo DuQuette (York Beach, ME: Samuel Weiser, 1993), p. 143.

[9] In this temple arrangement the quarters were determined by the cardinal signs of the zodiac; Aries (fire) in the east; Capricorn (earth) in the south; Libra (air) in the west; and Cancer (water) in the north.

evocation. Admittedly, it was a crude and unimaginative ritual, but at the time I thought it was pretty good.

It is here that I must point out a curious side effect that this ritual seemed to produce. On the first night of the ceremony an irritating drip developed in our bathtub which, because of our unresponsive landlord, developed within three days into a torrent. The irritation was compounded by the ear-splitting high frequency hiss the bathroom pipes emitted as all this water poured out of the faucet. While plumbing problems are hardly indicative of magical phenomena, the timing of the event caused me to joke with Constance that in reaction to all my fire invocations, the spirits of water seemed to be attacking the house. The waterfall in the bathroom grew louder and more maddening throughout the entire two-week operation. On the seventh night a thick marine fog rolled into the neighborhood and repeated its nightly visit for three straight evenings.

Finally the night of the final grand climactic consecration ceremony arrived. Each preceding night I worked myself up a little more, increasingly losing myself in ever wilder barbarous babbling. I was really getting behind this kind of magick. On the final night, with fourteen rounds of barbarous words, I was prepared to go all out.

As usual, Constance and Jean-Paul retired to the bedroom. I set up the living room temple as I had done for thirteen evenings. I got out the red bag that would be my wand's new home from that night forward. I put on my black robe, lit the bowl of alcohol and set to work.

Things were cooking. After all these nights I had everything memorized and flowing out of my mouth like Shakespeare. I could see the angelic guardians in the quarters, I could actually feel the fire as I ripped open the veils of spirit active and slashed the flaming pentagrams into place in the greater invoking ritual. By the time I began the barbarous words—AR-O-GO-GO-RU-ABRAO SOUTOU MUDORIO—I was a fire-spitting wizard with one thing on my mind, evoking the spirits of fire into my new wand. I was having the time of my life. I repeated the words again and again. It kept getting better—PhALARThAO OOO AEPE!

Suddenly I heard what sounded like rain on the roof, falling in loud heavy drops, then splattering on the driveway. Then the front our apartment shook as a great rushing hiss blasted against the front door. I stopped the ritual and looked out the window to see a thick geyser of water ejaculating five feet in the air in the middle of the driveway that separated the two rows of apartments. The main water line to the complex, a huge and ancient pipe, had burst underground right in front of our apartment and was washing chunks of asphalt into the street. All the neighbors were yelling and running out to see what was happening. Some had to quickly move their cars before they were swallowed by the rapidly forming sinkhole.

I stood there in my black hooded robe, clutching my magick wand, the living room illuminated wildly by the flickering light of a large flaming bowl of alcohol...

"My God! I can't let the neighbors see me like this!"

I quickly put out the flame, got out of my robe and joined the others outside as we waited for the Fire Department to arrive.

It was nearly 1 A.M. by the time things quieted down. I figured my wand had been concecrated enough. I performed a banishing ritual, closed the temple and put my newly consecrated wand in its new red bag. Already it had had quite a career. In the morning I would use it for the first time in my daily rituals.

Three hours later my alarm went off. It was still dark. I got up, washed my face and put on my black robe. I grabbed my new wand and put it on the living room chair. As I did every morning, I shuffled half asleep into the kitchen and fixed myself a short cup of coffee. A few minutes later I returned to the living room with my coffee and thoughtlessly sat down full force on my new wand—snapping it neatly in two.

CHAPTER 15

My Magick Wand —A Postscript

I debated for just an instant about how I was going to react. I came to the conclusion that if I didn't think this was funny I was unworthy to call myself a magician. I started to laugh. It was funny beyond funny. My laughter woke up Constance. It woke up Jean-Paul. I woke up the neighbors with my howls.

I didn't even consider gluing it back together. A weapon of Will that needs to be glued together is pretty damned pathetic. I asked my little family if they would let me have one more night alone in the temple.

That night's ritual was very simple. I banished and opened as usual. I lit the bowl of alcohol and placed the two broken pieces of my beautiful broken wand in the flames. Once they were burning I got out my naughty stolen surrogate wand that had served me so well the last few months. I passed it through the flames until the pieces of the broken wand were completely consumed. Just before the flame flickered out I stuck the tip of my old/new wand directly upon the dying ember and uttered my only words of invocation.

"Jump in there goddamn it!"

CHAPTER 16

Evocation of Orobas[1]

As I mentioned in the last chapter, Qabalistic tradition divides the human soul into four parts: Nephesh (the animal soul), Ruach (the intellect), Neschamah (the divine soul-intuition), and Chiah (the life force). Because we are "created in the image of God," these four parts reflect microcosmically the four qabalistic worlds that emanate from the great macrocosmic deity named Yod-Heh-Vau-Heh. In other words, my soul and your soul are miniature versions of the great soul of god—"as above, so below."

Theoretically, this means we all possess the same creative potential as our huge and vaporous counterpart. However, what keeps most of us from exercising our omnipotent prerogatives and doing god-like mischief is the unfortunate fact that there is a complete breakdown of communication between the four parts of our soul.

---

[1] For a brief summary of this tale see *Aleister Crowley's Illustrated Goetia,* by Lon Milo DuQuette and Christopher S. Hyatt, Ph.D., illustrated by David P. Wilson (Scottsdale, AZ: New Falcon Publications, 1992), p. 25.

We identify almost exclusively with Ruach and try to understand everything by means of our intellect. We disregard life-force, Chiah (which, in the final analysis, is probably our real identity) because the intellect alone cannot comprehend its profound subtlety. We are almost embarrassed when intuitive flashes from our Neschamah momentarily loosen the grip Ruach smugly holds on objective reality. Ruach even tries to rationalize the irrational tempests of our primitive animal soul.

Blinded by Ruach's limited scope of perception, we erroneously convince ourselves that the higher aspects of the Nephesh are simply the lusts and shortcomings of human nature. We cower in fear from the nightmarish demons of our lower Nephesh and attempt to exile them to the infernal regions of our personal (or denominational) hell, and herein lies the source of much pain and suffering.

Ironically, all four parts of the soul are already activated and fully functional, yet because Ruach tyrannically monopolizes the cosmic projector, we are stuck with thinking about the cosmic adventure instead of living it.

To remedy this unhealthy situation, the Eastern mystic ruthlessly assassinates Ruach and simply stops thinking. In Western ceremonial magick, however, we are not so anxious to throw the Ruach baby out with the bath water. Instead, we ritualistically encourage the four parts of the soul to talk to each other, thereby emulating the cooperation exhibited by the four interfacing qabalistic worlds (our giant counterpart). Once integrated, the parts of the soul become the perfect reflection of the divine world enabling the transcendent magician to wield the same immense power as the creative deity.

As a naive young magician, I was rudely introduced to the various parts of my soul during my first attempt to conjure a demon to visible appearance.

I had been in the O.T.O. for nearly a year and I was still unemployed. Our old car finally died and there was no money to replace it. Without transportation, job hunting in Southern California is almost impossible. I sold my piano and all but one of my guitars. The rent on our tiny apartment was paid through the month, but I had no idea where the next month's rent would come from. I still had a handful of guitar students who faithfully appeared once or twice a week to surrender five dollars to listen to an hour of my stories. Only the joy of being able to spend time with Constance and little Jean-Paul and my magical studies afforded me distraction from the grim realities of life as a starving *former* artist.

Among the texts recommended for my study was the First Book of the Lemegaton, *The Lesser Key of Solomon*, commonly called *The Goetia*.[2] Translated in 1888 by S. L. MacGregor Mathers (under the patronage of Aleister Crowley), this curious work is one of the most famous grimoires of all time. Perhaps its most notable claim to fame is its Preliminary Invocation that was picked up and used generically by the magicians of the Golden Dawn.

The bulk of the text is a description of seventy-two *fallen* angels who, having been tossed out of heaven for being insubordinate, are supposedly cooling their heels in hell.

The basic premise of Goetic evocation is this:

A skillful magician, using his or her "God-given" authority as a human being, can summon any spirit he or she wishes and compel it to obey any demand within its ability to perform. Some spirits are handy for destroying your enemies; others can get you a girlfriend, or discover treasure, or teach you medicine or astronomy or mathematics. (Upon reading the descriptions of this talented crew for the first time I noted in my diary: "No wonder Western religions are so stupid.

---

[2] *The Goetia, The Lesser Key of Solomon the King*, trans. Samuel Liddell MacGregor Mathers, edited, annotated, introduced, and enlarged by Aleister Crowley. Most recent edition edited by Hymenaeus Beta (York Beach, ME: Samuel Weiser, 1995).

There's been a brain drain!") The book contains detailed operating instructions complete with conjurations, constraints, curses (in case the spirits are uncooperative) and diagrams of each spirit's unique seal.

Although the Goetia is recommended *reading* for beginning students, Goetic evocation is usually reserved for more adept and experienced magicians. Predictably, the thought of conjuring up a demon to help me get my material life together was a very attractive prospect. I wrote my superior in the Order and told her how absolutely awful my material affairs were and that I was thinking seriously about evoking a Goetic spirit to help me out.

She wrote back and lectured me in no uncertain terms that Goetic evocation was "low magick" and I was not ready for such an operation; that it was dangerous and reckless, and if I needed a job why didn't I just "go out and get a job?" She counseled me to continue with my yoga and preliminary magical practices and forget about evocation until I achieved Knowledge and Conversation of my Holy Guardian Angel.

I knew she was right, and I certainly respected her advice. Still, it was obvious from her letter that she did not realize how desperate I really was. How could I stay focused on my spiritual practices when the future of my little family was at stake? I wrote her again. This time I simply asked, "Have you ever performed a Goetic evocation?"

"Certainly not," was her answer. "That's low magick."

Out of respect for my superior, I did not schedule an evocation. On the other hand, I did not feel that I would be too recalcitrant if I hypothetically selected a suitable spirit and started gathering up all of the equipment and accoutrements that would be necessary for such an evocation (should I ever decide to do it).

The spirit I selected was number fifty-five on the list of spirits, Orobas. The text read:

> *He is a Great and Mighty Prince, appearing at first*
> *like a Horse; but after the command of the Exorcist*
> *he putteth on the Image of a Man. His Office is to*
> *discover all things Past, Present, and to Come; also to*
> *give Dignities, and Prelacies, and the Favour of*
> *Friends and Foes. He giveth True Answers of Divin-*
> *ity, and of the Creation of the World. He is very faith-*
> *ful unto the Exorcist, and will not suffer him to be*
> *tempted of any Spirit. He governeth 20 Legions of*
> *Spirits.*[3]

For the life of me I couldn't see why on earth this fellow could be considered an "evil spirit."

He gives "dignities." Dignity was the very thing I lacked. I was in the humiliating and *un*dignified position of unemployment, poverty and starvation—I needed the "dignity" to provide adequately for my family!

He gives "prelacies." I had absolutely no idea what prelacies were, and frankly, at the time I didn't care.

He gives the "favor of friends and foes." Who couldn't use that?

He gives "true answers of divinity, and of the creation of the world." Just the magical tutor I needed for my study of the Holy Qabalah!

He is "very faithful unto the Exorcist, and will not suffer him to be tempted of any Spirit." That did it! This guy's perfect. Not only did it look like Orobas could help me pull my life together, he could also serve as a loyal familiar who would protect me from any nasty spirits who might want to mess with me.

In short order I had nearly everything I would need to operate. I could use masking tape to make a circle on the carpet in Jean-Paul's room. I made a posterboard triangle. Also

---

[3] *The Goetia*, p. 57.

Figure 2. Goetic Spirit Orobas. Illustrations from Author's diary.

out of posterboard, I made plaques with all the holy names I felt I would need to guard my circle. I had my almond wand and robe. For a mitre I would use a little blue yarmulke with the name of a local Jewish mortuary stamped on the inside.[4] I dutifully drew two sigils[5] of the spirit on beautiful paper. I had my hexagram of Solomon to pin to my black robe and I had prepared an outline order of ceremony and a customized conjuration to memorize.

Everything was ready except the Holy Oil, which I would need so I could anoint my head and consecrate my wand, the sigils,

---

[4] I had "forgotten" to take it off when I left services at the synagogue down the street.

[5] One sigil with the Tetragrammaton Pentagram inscribed on the reverse side is worn around the neck, the other is placed in the triangle of evocation and serves as the material basis for the spirit's appearance.

Figure 3. Sigil of Goetic Spirit Orobas.

and other temple furniture. For some smug reason I had convinced myself that the ceremony would be doomed to failure if I used anything other than pure Oil of Abramelin.

The recipe for this exotic and spicy unguent was first revealed in the most infamous of all magical texts, *The Sacred Magic of Abramelin the Mage,* written in 1458 by Abraham the Jew.[6] Made up primarily of pure cinnamon oil (the stuff school children in my day used to soak toothpicks in and then torture their lips and gums with its blistering fire). Olive oil and small portions of oil of myrrh and galangal are also used in the recipe.

Today Oil of Abramelin is relatively easy to purchase from specialty labs. In 1976, however, you either made it yourself or were lucky enough to know someone who could. Fortunately for me a dear friend on the East Coast sent me a small vial of the precious fluid. I immediately tested it by rubbing the tiniest drop on the center of my forehead. Instantly my skin burned like fire and left a light pink inflammation that lasted several hours. This was the real stuff. I was ready to whip up demons. Predictably, my excuse for doing so was directly forthcoming.

Two of my most dependable students (one half of my weekly income) were forced to stop their guitar lessons. Within days there would not even be enough food in the house. Things had to

---

[6] *The Book of the Sacred Magic of Abra-Melin, the Mage,* trans. S. L. MacGregor Mathers. (New York: Dover Publications, 1975).

change, and they had to change immediately. I believed that I was prepared to go to hell to make them change.

It was shortly after 2:00 in the afternoon. I told Constance and Jean-Paul to stay in the living room while I "did some magick" in Jean-Paul's room. I collected my weapons and laid them out on Jean-Paul's bed. I quickly taped out the circle and laid down the divine names. I set up a small incense burner in the triangle along with the seal of the spirit.

When everything was ready, I stripped and went into the adjacent bathroom and took a long shower while I recited the obligatory words, "Thou shalt purge me with hyssop, O Lord! and I shall be clean: Thou shalt wash me, and I shall be whiter than the snow." After drying myself, I put on my robe and dutifully chanted, "By the figurative mystery of these holy vestures I will clothe me with the armour of salvation in the strength of the Most High." I then uncorked the vial of Oil of Abramelin and dabbed the fingers of my left hand. I anointed my almond wand with the oil and rubbed it until it glistened with a warm even sheen. I then poured a little oil on the top of my head and put on my yarmulke. I dabbed my fingers once more in oil and anointed my forehead at the Ajna chakra.[7]

I looked around to assure myself that everything was in place and ready. I lit the incense and stepped into the circle. I was very nervous—no, I was very afraid. I performed the banishing rituals of the pentagram and hexagram. I was so unfocused that I felt it necessary to do them again.

I took a couple of deep breaths and tried to bolster myself with righteous self-affirmations. I wanted to convince myself, like ancient conjurers, that I had the divine right to do what I was doing. I repeated the short litany of my magical mottoes and the presumptuous titles of my formal degrees and then recited the Preliminary Invocation of the Goetia.

---

[7] The Third Eye.

That made me feel a little better. It is a very powerful enchantment.

I didn't believe it was necessary to blindly parrot the traditional conjurations so I customized one of my own using what I considered to be the essential formulae. It was short, much shorter than the long-winded ramblings in the Lesser Key of Solomon. It incorporated the barbarous words of evocation from the Preliminary Invocation, which I repeated in four rounds, one for each element and quarter. I had it all nearly memorized and was pleased with how it rolled off my tongue.

I unfolded my handwritten conjuration and began to recite. I recited it four times, each round louder and more intense. At the conclusion of the fourth round I was quite worked up. I looked up and gazed into the incense smoke arising from the triangle.

Nothing happened. I repeated all four rounds of the conjuration, this time with a bit more passion. I was sweating and already starting to tire. Still nothing. I hadn't prepared a second and stronger conjuration because I knew if I had one prepared I would be obliged to use it.

I stood in the circle in my black robe that pinched my armpits and that funny little skullcap and stared into the empty triangle.

I hated myself. I hated the whole momentum of my existence that had brought me to that ridiculous moment. I drew in an enormous breath and exhaled a sigh of hopeless depression. I wanted to vomit but the ache was too deep to purge. I slapped the palm of my hand with the magick wand and cursed myself.

"Look at you. You're a grown man with a wife and a child. You can't even feed them. How will you pay the rent? You don't even have a car to live in. You've sold everything; your guitars, your piano. You've no job. You've no hope. You're an idiot! Is this the only plan you can come up with to save your family?—to conjure a *genie* to come rescue you? You're pathetic, you're a failure; a failure in life, now you're a failure in magick."

I started hitting my hand harder and harder.

"It's your own damned fault. You're lazy! You've always been lazy. You think you're so special that the world owes you everything. You want to be rich but you can't make a dime. You dream of being famous, but what have you ever done to deserve fame? You let your music career slip through your fingers because you are too lazy to do any real work, too afraid to pay any real dues. You're a quitter. You're a loser! You've always been this way. Every chance you have ever had to make something of yourself you screwed up and blamed it on somebody else! But it's nobody's fault but yours!"

I started to quiver all over like I was about to explode. I broke out in a horrible sweat that stung every pore of my body. My scalp felt like I was wearing a cap of needles. I knew that I was having an emotional breakdown. Better here, I thought, instead of in front of Constance and Jean-Paul. I had come to the end of my rope. I stared blankly into the empty triangle, no longer with any thought of conjuration, but only as a place to nail my eyes as I crucified myself.

"It's your fault! It's your fault god damn you!"

The triangle became the pointed symbol of my laziness, of my stupidity, of my failure. It was the only clear object in the room.

"God damn you!"

I couldn't stop staring at the little piece of card stock.

"God damn you! God damn you! God damn you!"

I sank to my knees and whimpered. I had never felt so awful in my whole life. I wiped my nose on the sleeve of my robe and looked down at the disgusting silver streak. Suddenly my self-pity turned to rage. The emotional swing was so unexpected that it nearly took my breath away. I shook the wand wildly at the accursed triangle.

For the first time in my life I had something legitimate to blame all my troubles on—not the war, not my family, not my teachers, not my partner, or my wife, or the economy, or the government, or the church. Here at last was an object upon which I could spew all my frustration and fear. I had trapped the fiendish devil, the source of all my ills, in a cardboard triangle and it was going to listen to me. The monster was myself and my name was Orobas!

I ranted for what seemed forever before I came back to myself in the circle. I blinked and squinted through the tears and sweat and strained to see what was happening in the triangle. I didn't "see" anything, but something most definitely was happening. The feeling was unmistakable. I was no longer alone in the room. It was like waking up from an unsettling dream to discover that your dog is just inches away from your face staring at you.

I stood up and leaned forward for a better look. I was not prepared for this. I was only prepared for failure. The change of atmosphere in the room was unmistakable. I was paralyzed with wonder. I completely forgot the object of the operation. I knew without doubt the spirit was present in the triangle. I would soon have to deal with it. Second by second it became more tangible. I flushed with embarrassed confusion. It was really going to happen. I was about to meet a Goetic demon.

A large drop of sweat scurried from my scalp over my forehead and dripped into my right eye socket just below the bridge of my nose. It stung and made my eye water. I quickly wiped both my eyes with the fingers of my left hand. The powerful smell of cinnamon triggered a terrifying alarm. My hand and fingers were still covered with Oil of Abramelin! Like the biggest idiot in the world I had just rubbed sweat and concentrated cinnamon oil into both my eyes! A second later I was blinded by the most excruciating pain I have ever experienced. It was as though someone or something had jabbed red-hot pokers into my eyes.

I tried to open one eye then the other but the air exacerbated the agony.

"My God!" I thought, "This is the equivalent of a magical industrial accident." I spun around in the circle like a wounded animal. I couldn't leave the circle. It would break every rule of Solomonic magick. But what could be worse than this? I knew I had to get to the shower and rinse my eyes or I might never see again. With my eyes squeezed tightly shut I leveled my wand in the general vicinity of the triangle. "Stay!" I barked as if commanding a disobedient dog. "Stay there until I come back!"

As I stumbled blindly toward the bathroom door the most extraordinary thing occurred. I could see! I could see the whole scene as if I was perched somewhere in the ceiling. I saw myself moving toward the bathroom door with that stupid little beanie on my head. I saw the circle and the divine names. I saw the carpet, the windows, and the bed. I saw the triangle and inside the triangle, I saw the demon Orobas—a miniature black horse standing patiently. It had an almost comic oversized head with huge round eyes. It looked bored.

Under other circumstances I would have been awestruck by this clairvoyance, but it meant less than nothing to me. I was fighting to save my eyesight. I could care less about magick or demons or food or cars or rent or tomorrow.

As I lurched passed the triangle I shook my wand at Orobas and again shouted, "Stay!" The little horse obeyed by casually kneeling first on its front knees then dropping its hind legs and rump to the floor.

Inside the bathroom I stripped and blindly fumbled to find the cold water knob for the shower. I stuck my face into the icy stream and tried in vain to open my eyes. I had to hold them open with my fingers. I struggled to find the soap so that I could wash the Oil of Abramelin off my fingers. It seemed like it took forever. I carefully held both eyelids open with the thumb and forefinger of each hand and rolled my eyes madly to let the cold water pour over every inch of tortured eyeball.

I'm not sure how long I stood there. Eventually I was able to keep my eyes open without having to hold them open. I wept when I finally discovered I could see. The tears brought more relief to my eyes. The first thing I saw was my little blue yarmulke. It must have still been on my head when I got in the shower. It was plugging the drain and it was slurping loudly like a straw vacuuming the last drops of a giant milkshake. I pushed it away with my toe.

Reluctantly I turned off the water and stepped out of the tub. I caught my reflection in the mirror of the medicine cabinet. I looked like a demon. The "whites" of my eyes were bright blood red and shot with scores of tiny crows-feet veins. I had huge purple bags under my eyes and strings of snot clung to my mustache and beard. My hair stuck straight up and out over my ears forming an insipid crown of dripping spikes.

"Some wizard," I thought.

I reached into the tub and retrieved my magick cap. I put it back on my head without wringing it out. I again looked at myself in the mirror. I was wet and naked (except for my soaking yarmulke). I started to laugh. It felt good to see my demonic face smile. Then I really laughed—a great deep-breathed laugh that doubled me forward and left me hanging to the sides of the sink with both hands. I guess I had another emotional breakdown. This time it seemed like a healthy discharge of energy. It gave me a clean feeling of intense relief. I was very anxious to get back into the circle and talk to Orobas. I put on my robe, straightened my cap, picked up my wand and went back into the temple.

I didn't look into the triangle until I was back in the circle. I didn't "see" Orobas at all, but he was still there all right. I could tell because the triangle was still heavy with the smell of cinnamon, body odor, and fear.

I broke with tradition and sat down in my asana and addressed Orobas. I chose my words very carefully and whispered them slowly and clearly. To my surprise I "heard" his replies simultaneously, as if his answers rode upon the same mental wave that carried my words to him. Before I could finish asking him why he burned my eyes, he was already pointing out the fact that only an idiot would put cinnamon oil near his eyes in this heat.

I had to laugh and agree. I then continued with my original outline of questions. I first determined if Orobas was aware of the various powers attributed to him in the book, and if so, was he capable of exercising those powers. The answer being in the affirmative, I commenced to itemize the details of my predicament and charged him with the duty of immediately doing something to turn around my life.

"I will not presume to tell you how to go about it," I told him. "I do not intend to micromanage you or the spirits under your command. I only want it done now, within one hour of the end of this ceremony and you will do it without harming me, my family or friends or pets. Do you understand?"

He indicated that he understood, but even as I was giving him his orders I was thinking to myself how one hour isn't very much time to see some results. What if nothing happens? Then I'll be back in the same depressing position of failure. Perhaps I should give him a day or two to pull this miracle off—or a week— or a month—or six months! Something will most definitely happen within *six months* so I will be able to say to myself "It worked! Yes Lon! You're a successful magician!"

Then I stopped myself. No! Don't listen to him. This is not *me* talking, it's the damned spirit. That's how these guys operate. This imp has been counseling me my whole life with this kind of crap. This is exactly the kind of thinking that is screwing me up. No wonder demonic evocation has always been accompanied by tales of Faustian covenants and pacts with the devil. No!

This is where it stops! This is my chance to break this self-destructive cycle. That is precisely the reason I've got this little bastard in the triangle.

"Be still!" I said. "One hour and I meant one hour. If you serve me well I will carve your sigil in metal or stone that will last a thousand years, I will sing the praises of your great power and loyalty. Obey me, and I will be a kind and loving master. I will raise you spiritually even as I am raised. Help me to redeem myself and I will be the key to *your* redemption. But if you fail me I will conjure you only once more. And I will remember the pain in my eyes as I singe your sigils in the fire.[8] If you are not for me, you are against me, and I will not hesitate to annihilate you utterly!"

I don't know where I got the surge of righteous indignation, but this time it came straight from the heart. The words just poured from my mouth and the entire formulae of Goetic evocation fell into place. I felt like a magical grown-up.

Orobas immediately agreed. "One hour."

That was it. I had no more to say. I gave Orobas the license to depart as if I had recited it a thousand times. It included the standard stipulation that I could subsequently summon him at anytime without the heroics of a full formal conjuration. I banished the temple with the Pentagram and Hexagram rituals. I remained standing in the circle for a few minutes and waited for the "infernal" atmosphere in the room to dissipate. Orobas was gone.

I took the sigil out of the triangle and wrapped it and the other talismans in linen bags and put the triangle and divine names into a large envelope. I put my wand back into its red

---

[8] Before annihilating a disobedient spirit by completely incinerating its seal, Goetic magicians usually conjure it again for the purpose of torturing it into compliance. In the case of my first evocation of Orobas I was prepared, if he failed me, to jump straight to the ultimate penalty.

silk bag and changed into street clothes. I pulled up the tape circle and threw the sticky wad into the bathroom wastebasket and then threw every towel I could find on the bathroom floor to soak up the water. I looked at my reflection in the mirror. Did that really happen? My blood-red eyes confirmed that it did.

The temple was now once again just my son's bedroom. Just for good measure I repeated the banishing rituals and opened the door to the living room. Constance was busy in the kitchen and Jean-Paul was playing with his trucks on the living room floor. He looked up and giggled.

"Look at Papa's eyes!"

I mumbled something, then went to the kitchen to get a drink of water. It all seemed so unreal to me now. The details faded like early morning dreams when you become conscious of the fact that you are waking up. I stretched out on my back on the living room rug and struggled to reconstruct the chronology of events. This would have to go into my diary.

I closed my eyes just for a moment and realized how exhausted I was. I wanted to fall asleep, and I was drifting toward that golden moment of surrender when the painful roar of a mufflerless automobile shattered my peace, indeed, the peace of the entire neighborhood. We ran to the window to see an old rusted Chevrolet pulling up the driveway. It was dented in so many places and missing so much chrome that it was impossible to tell the year or model. To our terror it rolled directly up to our front door and stopped. The driver gunned the engine with one last smoky blast and turned it off.

It was Mad Bob. We hadn't seen him in two years. The last we heard was that he was in Guatemala with his girlfriend. (He hadn't written us but she did. The last letter from her said something like… "We just love it down here. Bob is teaching us to eat mosquitoes.") It was just like Bob to make an entrance like that. We were all very excited to see him.

We all endured his crushing hugs in the door and tried to pull him inside. He laughed maniacally (his trademark), but wouldn't be coaxed into a chair. Instead he threw his car keys at me and said, "The car's yours. Now you have to drive me back to Long Beach, I've got less than an hour to catch a ride back to Guatemala. What the f— happened to your eyes?"

He didn't give me time to answer. He pushed me into the driver's side of the old Chevy and we headed out down the Pacific Coast Highway to his rendezvous in Long Beach. On the way he did all the talking, telling me about the car's idiosyncrasies and secrets. He had me drop him off near downtown. As he got out he looked at his watch.

"Forty minutes. The old gal made pretty good time."

He pulled what looked like the pink slip for the car out of his wallet and told me to fill it out however I wanted.

"Thanks Bob. You don't know what this means to me!"

He giggled. "Sure I do."

We shook hands through the passenger window and he disappeared around a corner. I took a moment and looked around my "new" car. The floorboard was missing in places and I could look down between my feet and see the street. Almost every knob and door handle was missing. The horn worked; and the lights; and the radio. In the ashtray I found about sixty cents in change.

On the way home I stopped at a convenience store and used the change to buy an Orange County Register and a Three Musketeers Bar for Constance. Once home I tore into the "Help Wanted" section and circled three opportunities I could reach in my new car. I went to bed early and the next morning applied in person at all three. The third one, a medical device manufacturer, hired me on the spot.

At first my new job paid a little over minimum wage but I didn't care. My first payday was the following Friday. We bought groceries and at the end of the month I paid the rent. In a little over a month (as a reward for being the only person in my department dedicated enough to actually show up to work every day) they made me lead man of my section and a month later foreman of my department. That position lasted less than two months because I was promoted to the Quality Assurance lab and six weeks later asked to join the engineering department.

It has been over twenty years since that first evocation of Orobas. Obviously, I view it as a successful operation. That day was the pivotal moment of my adult life. As a matter of fact, it was the first day of my adult life. Mad Bob's gift of a car within the prescribed one hour was the unambiguous catalyst that triggered a chain-reaction of events that manifested everything that I demanded.

Dignities—Since the evocation I have enjoyed the "dignity" of being able to support and care for my family. I have also been singularly fortunate in my magical career. Within one year of the evocation I was given a great deal of responsibility in the O.T.O. which, over the years, has expanded considerably. I have tried to shoulder my duties with honor and dignity. I love the Order and consider my membership to be the single-most important factor in my magical reality.

Prelacies—A prelacy is a church office. A bishop is a prelate. On the same occasion I was honored with more responsibilities in the O.T.O. I was also, quite unexpectedly, consecrated Bishop in Ecclesia Gnostica Catholica, The Gnostic Catholic Church (the ecclesiastical arm of the O.T.O.). Several years later I was appointed Archbishop and was co-consecrated on three additional occasions.[9]

Favour of friends and foes—Over the years this has been particularly helpful. I have discovered that, more often than not, I do not have the good sense to recognize either a friend or a foe.

---

[9] This most recent consecration was at the hands of my dear friend and brother His Grace Tau Erigia as we visited Westminster Abbey, London.

It's much easier to enjoy the favor of both and not give a damn who's who.

True answers of divinity, and of the creation of the world— I continue to be a passionate student of the Qabalah (at least those aspects of the Holy Qabalah of interest to Hermetic magicians). I have written quite a bit on the subject and created a tarot deck incorporating various aspects of qabalistic magick.

*He is very faithful unto the Exorcist, and will not suffer him to be tempted of any Spirit—*For this service I remain perpetually grateful.

CHAPTER 17

Evocation of Orobas
—A Postscript

It is customary in Solomonic magick for the magician to hide the charged sigil of the spirit in a secret place. No one, except the magician, should touch the sigil or even look upon it. The theory is that the magician, having been protected from the malice of the spirit by the circle and holy names during the initial conjuration, remains so protected after the ceremony. However, any other person who may come in contact with the sigil is unprotected and totally vulnerable to the demon's influence.

After my first evocation of Orobas I put his parchment sigil in a small linen bag and put the bag inside my guitar. As I allowed no one to touch my precious C. F. Martin D-28, I thought that it would be supremely safe there. Also, I probably hoped that it might attract new guitar students or recording opportunities. Predictably, after a few weeks I forgot that I had put it there and did not give it another thought until after it was too late.

Kurt was a friend of one of my guitar students. He was a young man in his early 20s and a talented woodworker. His spe-

cialty was mother of pearl and abalone shell inlay. He showed
me photographs of his work and I was very impressed. He said
he would like to do some custom inlay on my Martin, in exchange for guitar lessons. This was an offer I could not refuse
and I greedily commissioned him to inlay an Egyptian winged
solar disk on the headpiece.

He told me he would need the guitar for a week. Five days
later he returned with the finished product. It was beautiful—a
fabulous job. I asked if he was ready to take his first lesson, but
he said he couldn't because he was going to accompany his father to the racetrack.

"Are you a race fan?" I asked.

"Not until yesterday," he said excitedly. "My dad and I spent
the whole day at Santa Anita. I just fell in love with the horses.
We went down by the paddock before each race to get a close
look. They're so beautiful. They're like gods. When they look at
me I feel like a horse!" He then whinnied like a horse.

Kurt's enthusiasm was almost embarrassing. He was obsessed
to the point of being creepy. Before he got on his bicycle to leave
he said. "Oh, while I was working on your guitar a little bag
dropped out. I opened it up and saw that little weird thing you
got in there. I thought I better not mess with Lon's magick weird
thing so I put it right back in the bag. It sure smells good. Hope
I didn't screw anything up."

I was stunned silent. Orobas got out. Now this guy thought
he was a horse.

"No." I lied to him, "I just put it in there to make my guitar
smell like cinnamon."

What could I tell him?

Kurt stayed part of our magical scene for the next fifteen
years, during which time he constructed many of our magical
tools and pieces of lodge furniture. Sadly, his addiction to
horseracing and other forms of gambling escalated year by year
into self-destructive behavior that eventually rendered him a so-

cial cripple. The last time I saw him he was living in a small industrial shop—the walls of his cell surrounded by hundreds of color photographs and posters of racehorses.

The reader may be asking at this point why I didn't conjure Orobas again and simply command him to leave Kurt alone? I did. On numerous occasions throughout the fifteen years we knew Kurt I conjured Orobas on the poor man's behalf. Each time my charge was, "If you are responsible for Kurt's behavior leave him in peace. If you are not the cause of his torment do what is in your power help him." Kurt's degeneration continued unabated.

I cannot think that accidental contact with a tiny piece of parchment was the cause of Kurt's ruin. Everything we know about the addictive personality suggests that sooner or later he was going to get caught up in something, be it drugs, or drink, or gambling. Though science and medicine may speculate upon physiological causes, and psychiatry may point to childhood experiences and trauma, and organized religion may blame man's inherent wickedness, all, in my opinion, fall pitifully short of a satisfactory explanation to the awful curse that tormented Kurt.

As I said in the introduction to this book, Magick is an art. If science, medicine, and religion cannot really answer these questions, why can't we be poetic when considering such mysteries and our inability to understand them? Perhaps the chemical imbalance in Kurt's blood—perhaps his mother's cold rejection—perhaps the monstrous doctrines of guilt and self-hatred heaped upon him year after year from the pulpit—perhaps all these things united in a diabolical marriage that gave birth to an evil spirit—a demon horse who escaped its wizard just long enough to gallop madly into the vulnerable soul of a weak and tragic human being.

CHAPTER 18

Israel Regardie and the Exorcism of Garkon

Early in 1980 I secured a comfortable position as a laboratory technician at yet another medical device laboratory. I was very lucky to work for a dear woman who was absolutely fascinated with my extra-curricular magical activities. One morning she burst into the lab and gushed, "Lon, pick up line two. It's a *Dr.* Regardie and he wants to speak to *Bishop* DuQuette."

Israel Regardie was my hero, a true adept and a living page of magical history. He was Aleister Crowley's secretary and student in the 1920s and later went on to rend the veil of the Golden Dawn with his controversial publication of its ceremonies and teachings. His books are the indispensable core of every English-speaking magician's library. He lived about sixty miles away in Studio City. Constance and I had been introduced to him a few years earlier by Grady McMurtry, the Caliph of the O.T.O. I had met with him only twice since then and we exchanged a few letters concerning a peculiar project dear to both of us.[1]

---

[1] As we both had collections of letters from individuals claiming to be incarnations of Aleister Crowley, I suggested we pool our stories and

This phone call was obviously a joke. Regardie had a play-fully twisted sense of humor. A few weeks earlier he had donated a box of books to Heru-ra-ha Lodge and I was sure he was call-ing to tell me he had more.

"Lon, this is Francis Regardie. Dear boy, I hope I haven't gotten you fired." He didn't mean it.

"Oh, everyone here knows I'm crazy." I didn't mean it.

"I was wondering if you could do me a bit of a favor. I need a bishop. As I'm sure you know, it takes a bishop to order an exorcism."

Now I really knew he was joking. I solemnly deepened my voice in mock virility. "Why yes Doctor, of course, naturally. How many exorcisms shall I put you down for?" I smiled and winked at my boss.

My smile quickly faded as I realized that he was not joking. As it turned out a psychiatrist friend of his was treating a patient who was convinced that she needed a formal exorcism. The woman was knowledgeable enough to know that classic exor-cisms must be performed under the direct auspices of a bishop with legitimate apostolic lineage.

"Your line is as good as any and I'm sure we can't get a *Christer* to cooperate on such short notice. Of course, she just needs a show. I thought you might know someone in your lodge who can give her one."

I couldn't believe he was asking me to do this. I giggled ner-vously and mumbled something.

"It's really quite sad actually. If you're up to it, you will need to talk with her doctor, do you have a pencil?"

Before I had the presence of mind to protest or ask any more questions he dictated the name and number of a Dr. Kaufman in

---

(cont.)
publish them as *Liber Nutz*. He liked the idea and sent me on several field trips to interview new Crowleys as they surfaced.

Long Beach. Before I hung up I reminded him that he, too, was a Wandering Bishop and asked why he didn't arrange the exorcism.

"I just did. Do tell me how it goes." He hung up.

A few minutes later I called Dr. Kaufman. She was a pleasant sounding woman who was very serious about scheduling an exorcism. Regardie had been her Reichian therapist and she admired him passionately. Although she made it quite clear she did not believe in demons and spirits other than as psychological metaphors, she was familiar with the fundamentals of Hermetic thought and respected its potential in modern therapy. I didn't need to ask any questions. She started talking and was very candid.

The subject was a 38-year-old woman named Sharon. Her husband had recently committed suicide and she was left with three children ranging in ages from 11 to 16.

When she was 2 years old her stepfather began sexually molesting her on a regular basis. Early on in this monstrous cycle of abuse, Sharon created a make-believe guardian, a friendly dragon named Garkon, who came and delivered her to happy places while her little body was being violated. He helped her survive her nightmarish existence, and for years this double life kept her relatively sane. As she grew older, however, her champion's character began to change.

Shortly after she started school and began noticing boys, Garkon's rescues were spiked with random acts of petty cruelty; a sharp dragon nip on the tummy or an ill-tempered scratch on her face. Ironically, Sharon felt that she deserved these little punishments and suffered them gladly, for without question her fantasy life with Garkon was infinitely preferable to the nightly visitations from her stepfather.

The years of abuse finally ended when she was 14. Her stepfather lost his head completely in a skillful display of physical contortion requiring the use of the kitchen table, the big toe of his right foot and a ten-gauge shotgun. That night when Sharon went to bed she dared to fantasize a new life free of the horrors of her early childhood. She would no longer need Garkon to rescue her, indeed, Garkon was a reminder of everything she wanted to forget.

But Garkon did not go away. The next night he swept into Sharon's bedroom. He had grown to an enormous size and lost all vestiges of his old friendly countenance. He boasted that he had eaten her stepfather's head and vowed that no man would ever hurt her again.

"The dynamics are pretty simple," Dr. Kaufman said. "He torments her cruelly whenever *any* factor of sexuality enters a life equation."

In high school she avoided the dating scene altogether and concentrated on her studies. She married in her junior year of college, but because she could never enjoy lovemaking without arousing Garkon's wrath, the marriage was predictably an unhappy one. The ordeal of conceiving and bearing children was excruciating. She nearly died during each of her three pregnancies. She was perpetually nauseous and often lost consciousness. After the birth of her third child, she and her husband ended their sexual relationship altogether and for ten years Garkon slumbered.

The truce was shattered when Sharon's husband committed suicide after a business failure. Many old issues from her childhood resurfaced, including Garkon. This time she resolved not to face the problem alone. She sought out psychological counseling.

This act of spiritual independence enraged Garkon who, now sensing the danger to his very existence, was escalating his attacks and making Sharon's life unbearable. She contemplated suicide (an idea that Garkon wholeheartedly endorsed). Instead she settled on the idea of an exorcism.[2] Her psychologist would

---

[2] Ironically, Sharon was not a devoutly religious person. In fact, she fancied herself a New Age agnostic.

have none of it and referred her to Dr. Kaufman, thinking that at least a psychiatrist could prescribe appropriate medication. Dr. Kaufman resisted drug therapy but was willing to explore exorcism as a psychodramatic exercise.

I didn't know what to say. The story was very compelling. Dr. Kaufman seemed anxious that I appreciate the psychological significance of Sharon's "possession" and was patient enough to keep pointing out how all this was perfectly understandable from an analytical point of view.

I really wanted to help, but this was serious stuff. I could barely keep my own demons from eating me. I certainly did not feel equipped to exorcise such a formidable psychic entity from someone else. Still, it seemed as if the whole universe (and my magical hero) had conspired to put me in the middle of this situation. I thought for a moment who I might know among my eccentric and bohemian cronies who was knowledgeable enough (and crazy enough) to be my exorcist. The answer came to me immediately.

"I know who can do it if he will agree. When do you want this done?"

"Tonight," Dr. Kaufman answered as though she was sure I should have already known that, "at my home in Long Beach."

Nathan Sanders was an O.T.O. Brother and the most experienced Goetic magician I had ever met. He was the former student of Carroll (Poke) Runyon, the legendary master of the art of evocation.[3] Using classic and flawlessly memorized conjurations, Nathan could summon anything into his triangular black

---

[3] See *The Book of Solomon's Magick*, by Carroll "Poke" Runyon (Pasadena: Church of Hermetic Sciences, 1996). Runyon rediscovered the key secret of conjuring a spirit to visible appearance in the black mirror. This facial distortion technique had been lost in the middle ages, leaving a half millennium of magicians struggling to see spirits in the incense smoke rising from an empty triangle.

mirror, and his evocations were not limited to the seventy-two spirits of the Goetia. I had seen him conjure to visible appearance angels, elementals, and even historical and fictional characters.[4] He was truly an extraordinary magician and I was sure if anyone could make Garkon appear it was Nathan. (I guess I assumed he could also make him go away.)

As I expected, Nathan was only too happy to answer the Bishop's call and assume the role of exorcist. I called Dr. Kaufman again and told her the exorcism was on. Because of the distances involved it was nearly 10:00 P.M. before Nathan and I knocked at her door. We would have arrived an hour earlier, but our travel was hindered by a thick coastal fog.[5]

Dr. Kaufman greeted us cordially and apologized for the way the house smelled.

"We've had a difficult evening. Since I told Sharon we were doing this tonight, she hasn't been able to hold down any food. She lost her 7UP when she heard you knock."

Nathan and I did our best to appear unmoved and professional. Personally, I wanted out of there.

"Perhaps we should do this another time," I eagerly suggested.

"No, I expected worse actually. Garkon obviously doesn't want to say goodbye."

---

[4] Oddly enough, such acts are perfectly consistent with magical theory. The entities Bilbo Baggins and Santa Claus have for many individuals far more archetypal "reality" than the spirits one usually associates which this type of magical activity.

[5] I can hear you laughing. Yes, I said fog! I have no doubt that many readers will find it difficult, if not impossible to believe much of what I am now about to relate. To garner some small semblance of credulity, I even toyed with the idea of omitting many details that smack shamelessly of a Hollywood melodrama starting with an atmospheric cliché like a spooky, foggy night. But what can I say? I won't apologize. This event took place in Southern California where it often gets foggy that time of year.

She led us into the kitchen and introduced us to Sharon, who was sitting at the table with a can of soda and a cigarette in her hand. She was an attractive woman in jeans and a gaily-patterned ski sweater. Her complexion was pasty and she wore dark glasses that hid dark circles under her eyes. She thanked us for coming and asked what she would need to do. Nathan said he would like to first ask her a few questions. She agreed.

I was somewhat surprised by his questions. The first one seemed downright rude. He asked her if she was "addicted" to fantasy literature. Sharon smiled and said, "Why, yes, I guess I am."

He then asked details about Garkon's appearance—his shape, his color, did he ever color change, number of fingers, toes, eyes. Lastly, he asked her how to spell Garkon's name. On his notepad he carefully inscribed the letters of Garkon's name in Hebrew.

"Knowing the name of the spirit is the key to controlling the spirit." Nathan's delivery was dramatic and effective. "Bishop DuQuette is going to take these letters and construct the spirit's magical signature using a Kamea of Saturn.[6] We'll

---

[6] A kamea, or normal, magick square consists of the distinct Positive Integers 1, 2, ...$n2$, such that the sum of the n numbers in any horizontal, vertical, or main diagonal line is always the same. A kamea of Saturn is a square 3x3 (Saturn being attributed to the 3rd Sephirah of the Tree of Life. Kameas for the other planets are: Jupiter, 4x4, Mars, 5x5, Sol, 6x6, Venus, 7x7, Mercury, 8x8, and Luna 9x9. The Hebrew letter or letters numerically equivalent to the numbers can then be used to spell out any word or name. Garkon's sigil drawn on a kamea of Saturn.

4	9	2
D-M-Th	T-Tz	B-K-R
3	5	7
G-L-Sh	H-N	Z-Au
8	1	6
Ch-P	A-Y-Q	V(o)-S

then draw this sigil on the back of these pentagram talismans. In the ceremony each of us will wear one around our neck to link us to the spirit and remind him that we are his masters."

Nathan was assuming an awful lot when he announced I was going to do all of the sigil drawing. Fortunately for Bishop DuQuette's reputation, the magick square of Saturn (3x3—the smallest and simplest of all the planetary kameas) was the only one I could draw from memory. I whipped out those sigils like I knew what I was doing.

That was it for the interview. We spent the next half-hour bringing things in from the car. In addition to his beautifully constructed break-down magical circle and the triangular black mirror, we brought four black robes and every magical tool a well-equipped Solomonic magician would need: wand, sword, lamp, white-handled knife, black-handled knife, brass box of torment, talismans, holy water, salt, oil of Abramelin, incense, and candles.

Nathan told Dr. Kaufman and me to wash our hands and faces before robing up. As for himself, he would take a shower. When he reappeared from the bathroom he was decked out in his full magical regalia. I have to admit he looked every inch an exorcist.

He then presented Sharon the robe she would wear in the ceremony and instructed her to also shower and wash her hair thoroughly. It was nearly midnight before she came out of the bathroom. She had towel dried her hair and she looked like a frightened little girl.

There wouldn't be room for all of us in the circle of art, so we created a large outer circle with a length of clothesline. Sharon would stand in the central circle holding two lighted tapers. The triangular black mirror was placed outside of both circles and positioned so that she could easily see the reflection of her own face illuminated by the candles. Nathan, also in the central circle, stood directly behind her. He would be the "operator" and she the "receiver." Dr. Kaufman and I were to stand in the outer circle on either side and slightly behind Sharon. We all had our sigil/ pentagram talismans around our necks and a parchment hexagram of Solomon pinned to the skirt of our black robes.

Nathan then ran through a quick checklist of items to see if all was in readiness. Was the phone off? Were the doors locked? Were the pets outside? Did anyone need to pee? When he was satisfied, he lit the two candles in Sharon's hands, and turned out all the lights. Before entering the circle to begin the ceremony he unwrapped a tiny cake of hotel soap and with it drew a large version of Garkon's sigil in the center of the black mirror. This act made Sharon gasp sharply as if someone had seized her throat. I was no longer nervous, I was afraid.

"Your Grace, would you be so kind as to banish the temple by the rituals of the pentagram and hexagram?" This was another one of Nathan's kind gestures to make it appear that I was needed. I didn't mind. At least it was something simple I could do to be helpful. After I banished, Nathan performed brief cleansing and consecration ceremonies and formally declared the temple open. He asked Sharon to take several deep breaths, relax and gaze at her reflection in the triangle. He then began to recite the classic conjuration of the Goetia.

> *I do invocate and conjure thee, O Spirit, Garkon; and being with power armed from the Supreme Majesty, I do strongly command thee...*

Nathan used a special voice for his conjurations. It was lower and stronger than his natural voice, but gave no hint of artificial affectation. His words rode smoothly upon two or three notes. Whenever the text ran into pockets of bizarre and unintelligible names and words he linked them smoothly into a sonorous string almost as if they were one long master word of unspeakable power.

> *...by Beralanensis, Baldachiensis, Paumachia, and*
> *Apologiae Sedes; by the most Powerful Princes, Genni,*
> *Liachidae, and Ministers of the Tartarean Abode; and*
> *by the Chief Prince of the Seat of Apologia in the Ninth*
> *Legion, I do invoke thee, and by invocating conjure thee.*

All the while he conjured he held his wand high and drew angelic sigils in the air above Sharon's head.

> *And being armed with power from the Supreme Maj-*
> *esty, I do strongly command thee, by Him Who spake*
> *and it was done, and unto whom all creatures be obedi-*
> *ent...*

He wasn't through the first section when Sharon started to weave back and forth and let out short pitiful sobs. Nathan went on but was soon drowned out by Sharon's whimpering. He continued louder and louder.

> *By all the names of God, Adonai, El, Elohim, Elohi,*
> *Ehyeh Asher Ehyeh, Zabaoth, Elion, Jah, Tetragramma-*
> *ton, Shaddai, Lord God Most High, I do exorcise thee*
> *and do fully command thee, O thou spirit Garkon, that*
> *thou dost forthwith appear unto us here before this Circle*
> *in a fair human shape, without any deformity or tortu-*
> *osity....*

Sharon was now thrashing from side to side sobbing uncontrollably. I was certain she was faking. She'd seen too many movies, I thought. I was embarrassed for her, embarrassed for all of us. The noise and commotion were too much for Nathan. He stopped reciting the conjuration and simply shouted at Sharon "Is the spirit in the triangle?"

"Yes!" Sharon screamed angrily. "He's *always* been there!"

When I heard those words, I knew she was not acting. I felt the hair on the back of my head spring to attention. The atmosphere in the room seemed to collapse under a crushing wave of primitive malice. I was petrified.

Sharon dropped her hands forward, spilling hot wax down the front of her robe and onto the carpet. I stepped forward and lifted her hands back into position. When I touched her arms, they were as hard as rock. Her wrists and hands were swollen to such a degree that her fattened fingers could barely close around the candlesticks. I stole a quick glance at her face. It was bright red and her cheeks so puffed up that her eyes were nearly pinched shut.

With the tip of his wand Nathan poked me back to my station and commenced to address the spirit. Even in this chaotic environment he calmly welcomed Garkon and praised him for all his years of service to Sharon when she was a little girl. He then explained that Sharon was now grown up and that his actions were hurting her.

Sharon stopped crying and began to let out an extended monotone howl of the word "no." She held the note until her breath was exhausted. As she pushed the last air from her lungs she induced a cycle of coughing that eventually led to retching spasms of dry heaves. Dr. Kaufman and I had to take the candles away from her. Nathan shouted at her. "Look into the triangle! Is Garkon in the triangle? Tell me what he is saying."

"Oh yes!" Sharon hissed with venomous sarcasm. "He's laughing at you!"

It soon became clear that Garkon could not be drawn into dialogue. The spirit's only response was to create terror and then feed on that terror. He was doing a very good job. Poor Sharon bobbed up and down like a caged monkey shifting from foot to foot as she gawked open-mouthed at the triangle. From where I stood it appeared that she no longer had a neck. Her shoulders had risen and become squared. I remember thinking that it looked like she had put on her robe with a coat hanger still in it.

Nathan tried once more to reprogram Garkon to become a supportive familiar but Garkon would have none of it. The response was always the same—more pain inflicted upon Sharon.

"Then, if you refuse to help her you will no longer be allowed to hurt her!"

Nathan popped the cork on the crystal vial of holy water and shook it—first upon Sharon and Dr. Kaufman and me, then upon the triangle itself.

> *Now, O Garkon, since thou art still pernicious and disobedient; I do in the name, and by the power and dignity of the Omnipresent and Immortal Jehovah Tetragrammaton do bind thee in the depths of the Bottomless Abyss.*

He emptied the vial of holy water over Sharon's head, then ripped the parchment talisman bearing Garkon's sigil from around her neck. He reached to where I stood with the lighted candle and passed the talisman through the flame.

> *I conjure thee, O fire, by him who made thee and all other creatures for good in the world, that thou torment, burn, and consume this Spirit Garkon, for everlasting.*

He then allowed the talisman to catch fire and held it until it was almost consumed. He tossed the last flaming fragment in the air. It burned completely out before it reached the floor. I was very impressed.

> *I hereby excommunicate thee, and destroy thy name and seal and burn thee in the immortal fire and bury thee in immortal oblivion.*

Predictably, Sharon howled and babbled. Nathan then stepped between her and the mirror and from the confines of the circle he hurled a black cloth at the triangle. It snagged the uppermost point and fell to cover the entire surface of the mirror. He turned Sharon away from the triangle and gently helped her to the floor. He raised his wand and aimed it at the covered mirror.

Christeos cormfa peripsol amma ils!
Let the company of heaven curse thee!
Christeos ror, graa, tofglo aoiveae amma ils!
Let the sun, moon, and all the stars curse thee!
Christeos luciftias od tofglo pir peripso amma ils, pujo
  ialprg ds apila, od pujo mir adphahtl!
Let the light and all the Holy Ones of Heaven curse thee,
  unto the burning flame that liveth forever and unto
  the torment unspeakable!

Nathan sat down beside Sharon and put his arms around her. We all remained silent for what seemed like a long time. He then helped her to her feet and showed her the mirror.

"That's it," he said cheerfully. "All gone. You'll never be this embarrassed again. Thank you for not throwing up on my robe."

Sharon laughed and hugged him. We all laughed and hugged.

"Your Grace, will you do the honors?" Nathan really enjoyed his role as exorcist. He had done a fantastic job. I was so proud of him—so proud of all of us. I quickly performed the banishing rituals of the pentagram and hexagram, after which Nathan closed the temple. The entire ceremony took a little less than an hour.

We were all in high spirits. Dr. Kaufman told Sharon that during the ceremony she had blown up like a blimp. I was relieved to learn that I wasn't the only one to notice the phenomenon. Dr. Kaufman apologized for forgetting to tell me that for years Sharon's joints swelled dramatically during Garkon's attacks. In fact it was these physical manifestations that first attracted her to the case.

It was two weeks before I heard back from Dr. Kaufman. In her opinion the operation was a success. Garkon seemed to be out of Sharon's life, and she was making progress on all other levels of her therapy.

I called Nathan and we crowed like self-congratulatory cocks. I then called Regardie and tried not to sound too excited. He said that he had already talked with Dr. Kaufman and she had praised us "to high heaven." He was happy that it worked out but he cautioned me about celebrating prematurely. His parting words left me a bit uneasy.

"The law of conservation of energy applies to magick as well as physics. Our friend may not have been destroyed, he may have just moved along to the nearest center of least resistance."

This was the last time Regardie and I spoke. Two years later I would receive another call from Dr. Kaufman and a new lesson in the conservation of energy.

CHAPTER 19

The Exorcism of Garkon
—A Postscript

Two years to the month after Sharon's exorcism Dr. Kaufman called me again to see if Nathan and I would be willing to help Sharon.

"Not Garkon again!" I groaned.

"No," she laughed. "Actually Garkon has been gone since the exorcism. Sharon finished her master's degree and is now a Ph.D. candidate at UCLA. No, Sharon's doing great. There's been a family tragedy, though. Her son Robert committed suicide day before yesterday and the two girls are taking it pretty hard."

This didn't sound like anything that should involve the esoteric theatrics of Bishop DuQuette's traveling demon show. I voiced my sadness and asked Dr. Kaufman to relay my sympathy. I knew etiquette now demanded I say something like... "*Is there anything I can do to help?*" but I resisted the temptation to be a gentleman. I could feel Dr. Kaufman waiting for me to say it and for several uncomfortable moments we remained locked in a showdown of silence.

"Lon, maybe you can give me some advice."

Oh god! I didn't know what was coming but I knew I wasn't going to like it.

"Alex, Sharon's oldest girl, believes her brother's ghost is having sex with her."

Why did I answer the phone? I sat down and pushed off my shoes. "Go on."

The story she related was every bit as bizarre and gruesome as Sharon's possession. In fact, as Dr. Kaufman unfolded the details I couldn't help but view the scenario from a magical perspective and the conclusions I drew made me sick at heart.

For nearly their entire lives Sharon's three children were forced to grow up with a suicidal father and a mother who was perpetually on the brink of madness. In this unwholesome environment they had only themselves to turn to for emotional support. As bright kids, they soon discovered what keys to turn and what buttons to push to exploit their dysfunctional parents. In a nutshell, as long as mom and dad were crazy the kids got anything they wanted out of them.

Their father's suicide and their mother's liberation from Garkon changed all of that almost overnight. Sharon now had her life back and was not about to return to the old insane patterns, including allowing herself to be manipulated by three disturbed and very spoiled children.

The two oldest, Robert (now 18) and his sister Alex (now 16) acted out their frustration in grand style by publicly flaunting their heretofore-secret incestuous relationship. Their reputations ruined at school, Robert enlisted in the Air Force and Alex plunged headlong into nymphomaniacal promiscuity.

After less than a month of basic training, Robert went AWOL and came home. In one last attempt to bring Sharon back into line he accidentally hanged himself in the garage in what the coroner called a "failed *mock* suicide attempt." For the two days and nights since her brother's death Alex had been violently masturbating in her room "smothered," as she moaned, "in Robert's embraces."

I really didn't want to get involved in this one, but really had very little choice in the matter. I called Nathan who reluctantly agreed we should go and at least banish the house. I also invited Deborah Weiner, a mutual friend and gifted clairvoyant.

At Sharon's home we asked first to see the garage where Robert died. To our shock and utter disgust the area had not been touched since the body had been removed. The remains of the severed rope still draped from the ceiling beam and the floor was still covered with the foul contents of the poor boy's bowels.

We then toured the rest of the house including Robert's bedroom. His bed was still unmade and his unwashed laundry was strewn all over the floor. The three of us huddled for a few minutes and decided the first thing that needed to be done was to rid the house of everything to which the shell of a confused and recently disembodied person might be attracted. The first things to go would be the filthy sweat-soaked clothes to which the throbbing residue of his vital essences still clung like Spanish moss. Barbara said there was enough astral chum in the air to build the bodies of fifty ghosts.

We cleared out his room completely and piled all of his dirty clothes, his bathroom towels and his sandy wet-suit on the floor of the garage. We then proceeded to ceremonially banish and cleanse every room in the house except the garage. Our plan was to lure Robert out of the house and concentrate him in the garage. Before we dealt with Robert in the garage however, we needed to talk with Alex.

Alex behaved as if she didn't want to be banished, or exorcised, or bothered. We respected her wishes. She did allow us to banish and cleanse her room, and before we left her she cooperated in a little ceremony Nathan had devised. He tied one end of a length of string around a portrait of Robert and the other around Alex's waist. He then gave her a pair of scissors and asked her if she could cut the string. She said she could and proceeded to do so.

Our last duty was in the garage and included (along with a lot of bell ringing) the supreme banishing rituals of the pentagram and hexagram and the whole spectrum of Golden Dawn purification and consecration ceremonies.

Sharon thanked us and vowed that she would get rid of everything in the garage the next day. As we shook hands I realized that Regardie was right. Garkon had just moved along to the nearest center of least resistance. I didn't want to know where the law of conservation of energy would send him from here.

Chapter 20

Enochian Spirits—First Worshipper, Friendly Visit

The lodge was growing steadily and the new members were understandably anxious to meet and study magick. I scheduled a weekly class in our home and began organizing my thoughts concerning the fundamentals of magick. It was finally sinking in that there were some people in the world who actually knew less about the subject than I.

The class was attended by some very bright people[1] and in short order I realized that in order to stay one jump ahead of them I was going to have to study very hard and be resourceful. By the time we mastered the pentagram and hexagram rituals, and had consecrated our elemental weapons, it was clear I was going to have to come up with some-

---

[1] My role as class master was more as host and moderator. Several members of class were already far more knowledgeable than I in astrology and other occult sciences. With nostalgic pride I can tell you that alumni of this class have since become celebrated luminaries of our modern occult/magical subculture, including the deliciously diabolical S. Jason Black.

Author (with shaved head) with noted diabolist S. Jason Black.

thing dramatic. I combed my *Gems from the Equinox*[2] for something exotic and different and turned to *Liber Chanokh: A Brief Abstract of the Symbolic Representation of the Universe Derived by Doctor John Dee Through the Skrying of Sir Edward Kelley.*[3] It was full of magick squares, charts, diagrams, and a series of "Calls" in a strange angelic language. If the class

---

[2] *Gems From the Equinox: Instructions by Aleister Crowley for His Own Magical Order.* Israel Regardie, ed. Most recent edition (Scottsdale, AZ: New Falcon Publications, 1992), p. 385.
[3] Between 1582 and 1589 Dr. John Dee (1527–1608), English Magus and mathematician and astrologer to Queen Elizabeth I, together with clairvoyant Edward Kelley (1555–1597), in an attempt to communicate with the angelic hosts of God [as did the Patriarch, Enoch—hence the term Enochian], involved themselves in an amazing series of magical workings. Their efforts yielded a wealth of magical information, including a detailed dissection of the phenomenal and spiritual worlds, and an angelic language used to evoke particular spirits and access

wanted exotic, this certainly looked like it. At our next meeting I announced that we would soon begin a six-week Enochian Magick workshop.

At the time the material in *Gems* and Regardie's *Golden Dawn*[4] was the only information I had on the Enochian system. I read through the texts several times and came to the conclusion that I would understand the material better if I constructed the various pieces of Enochian equipment. These consist primarily of four Elemental Tablets, one each for Fire, Water, Air, and Earth, and one smaller Tablet of Union (or Spirit Tablet). Each Elemental Tablet is composed of 156 truncated pyramids. Each pyramid (or square) is lettered on top and each of the four sides is colored to represent an element, planet, or zodiacal sign.

Each pyramidal square is home to an angel or spirit whose characteristics are determined by the specific elemental mix as indicated by the colors on its sides. The letter on the top of the pyramid is the angel's name (or a letter in the name of a larger angel).

For example: if a pyramid lettered "A" is colored yellow (Air) on two sides and blue (Water) on the two other sides, it houses an elemental being named "A" whose character and scope of intelligence is defined by (and limited exclusively to) the elemental "natures" of Air and Water. Using the classic elemental images of the Kerubic beasts (Lion=Fire; Eagle=Water; Human=Air; and

---

(cont.)
the various levels of heaven. Dee kept copious notes many of which survive today. Much Enochian material was incorporated in the Golden Dawn's Adeptus Minor program. Crowley's *Liber Chanokh* was a digest of this material. See *Enochian World of Aleister Crowley*, by Aleister Crowley, Lon Milo DuQuette, Christopher S. Hyatt, Ph.D. (Scottsdale, AZ: New Falcon Publication, 1991).
[4] *The Golden Dawn.* Israel Regardie, ed. (St. Paul: Llewellyn Publications, 1992).

Bull=Earth)[5] angel "A" could be symbolically represented as a sphinx with a man's head and body (for Air) and an eagle's wings and legs (for Water). Obviously, such an elemental spirit would have a very narrow range of duties in the universe. On the material plane, these duties might regulate the behavior of clouds or mists. In the human psyche they may play a specific part in the dynamics of our emotional life.

Then let's say that right next to angel "A" lives angel "B" who is half Earth (black or green) and half Fire (red). Angel "B" would naturally have drastically different characteristics than angel "A". (Using Kerubic images it would have the head and body of a bull (Earth) with the paws and legs of a lion (Fire).

Keeping this in mind we see that each Enochian Elemental Tablet has, first of all, 156 angels with one-letter names, and very specific attributes and responsibilities in the universe. However, we do not stop here. Enochian elemental spirits are modular. They fit together just like the elements fit together in infinite combinations and ratios to create the phenomenal universe. Angel "A" can join with its neighbor angel "B" to create angel "AB" whose characteristics are more complex than either "A" or "B" alone. Angel "AB" in turn can join with other squares to form bigger and even more intricate beings, etc.

The more I learned about the Enochian system, the more thrilled I became at its divine perfection. The laws that dictate the ordering of the elements and the organization of the squares are examples of Hermetic logic at its most sublime.

The class was enthralled. Most members set to work painting their own set of tablets. As complex as the process appears to be at first, the simple act of coloring the tablets makes the method-to-the-madness easy to understand. In the meantime, I

---

[5] The four beasts of the vision of Ezekial representing the Kerubic or fixed signs of the zodiac—Leo/Fire/Lion, Scorpio/Water/Eagle, Aquarius/Air/Human, Taurus/Earth/Bull.

was determined to build a full set of three-dimensional Enochian tablets. (Up until this time Enochian magicians simply drew the pyramids on a flat surface.) I mentioned my plan to Dr. Regardie who counseled strongly against it. "They're dangerous enough when they're flat!" he cautioned. "Don't give them dimensional elbow room."

As much as I respected the good doctor I really didn't see how it would hurt to fully manifest the tablets in 3D. In fact, I thought, maybe the reason Regardie's Enochian spirits were so crabby was because he had them all squished into those flat tablets.

I commissioned Kurt, who owned a table saw, to cut 644 wooden truncated pyramids with one-inch bases. I bought sandpaper, sealant and acrylic paints. As soon as the pyramids were cut I went to work like a man possessed. I got up early in the morning to sand, seal, and paint. I became totally engrossed in the project. Time lost all meaning to me. Each morning I found myself arriving at my job later than the morning before. The tablets were all I could think about. Each day I stole away from work a little earlier so I could get home to sand, seal, and paint. Soon I was sanding and sealing and painting all day long because I no longer *had* a job to distract me. I didn't care. The tablets were indescribably beautiful. I was so proud. I finished the small Tablet of Union first, then the Elemental Tablet of Earth. I couldn't wait until the other tablets were finished. I was determined we would try out the Earth tablet at the next class.

Up until this point, my only experiences with spirit evocation had been of the Goetic/Solomonic variety. I did not have a clue what to expect from an Enochian working, and I was particularly unsure how to proceed in a group setting. Mercifully, there was no ambiguity about the technical procedures. Temple openings, Enochian Calls, and the angelic hierarchies were all laid out quite clearly in *Liber Chanokh*. I performed a series of experimental evocations (a Kerub from each of the four tablets) before retiring on four consecutive nights. I made note of my dreams and concluded that this kind of work was harmless and effective.

For our first evocation session I decided we would work as Dee and Kelley did. One person would act as seer, and one as operator. The seer would recite the appropriate call, receive the vision and communicate it during or after the session. The operator would banish, open and close the temple, and question the seer. I would be the operator, but I did not know who in our little class would be the first to sit in the visionary driver's seat. On class night there was only one rather reluctant volunteer.

David P. Wilson was not new to the world of magick. In the years leading up to his affiliation with our lodge he sat in with a host of magical groups and workshops in the Los Angeles area upon whom he later heaped scorn and ridicule because of their inability to show him "real magick." He was the boldest member of the class, also the most impatient and sarcastic. I could see the Enochian class going down in flames on opening night because David the curmudgeon once again "saw nothing!" He had done none of the preliminary Enochian work with the rest of the class. He hadn't painted a set of tablets or studied any of the calls. Still, he was our only volunteer.

I can't recall why, but I decided we would to try to contact LAIDROM, the Mars Senior[6] of the Elemental Tablet of Earth. In the spirit of *better safe than sorry,* we placed the Earth tablet in the South (Capricorn/Cardinal Earth) and enclosed the entire class in a circle cast with a clothesline cord. I banished with the rituals of the lesser and greater pentagrams and hexagrams, then opened the temple and invoked the hierarchical names as indicated in *Liber Chanokh.* David was seated on the floor at the

---

[6] Each Elemental Tablet has a Solar King and six Planetary Seniors. These seven spirits are very high on the Enochian hierarchical ladder. Their Names are drawn from the squares of the great cross that separates each Elemental Tablet in to four sub-divisions (subangles).

southern edge of the circle just inches away from the Earth tablet. Leaning against the wall behind the tablet was a huge cardboard version of the Tablet of Earth that I placed there for the other members of the class to focus upon. I turned on the tape recorder and gave David a copy of the Call to read. I sat down behind him while he read it aloud.

He did rather well considering he had never read it before. When he was finished he closed his eyes and took a deep breath. Nothing happened. I asked him to read the Call again. He did so and after only a few seconds he said, "I have a landscape. I see a landscape."

I was relieved beyond words. "What does it look like?"

David proceeded to describe in surprising detail a desert vista of flat, trackless white crystalline powder stretching to the horizon. Great gray columns of volcanic rock towering over the plane broke the monotony of the scene. Between the columns the ground was pockmarked with countless gaping pits.

That was it. Nothing else was occurring. I asked him to read the call a third time. This time there was movement. From out of a pit in the center of his field of vision arose a black cone. He said it sparkled from the inside and upon its surface with thousands of little sparks that jumped from one star to another.

I asked, "Is this LAIDROM?"

David grabbed his pencil and notepad and quickly scribbled something. I looked at what he had drawn. It looked like four very poorly drawn Enochian letters. At the time it meant nothing to me. I asked for a clearer answer. "Is this LAIDROM?"

"It's him! It's him! I see him."

He described a humanoid figure draped in the same material from which the cone was constructed. He had an egg-shaped head but no face. His hands were like mittens—there were no fingers. He reached his arm toward the ground and "drew" a diagram in the sand in front of him. David quickly copied the figure on the notepad. It was a square divided diagonally by two lines with a small circle in the lower left-hand corner. We took this to be LAIDROM's signature.

We were all very excited. It was as if the entire class saw David's vision in our mind's eye. Then it occurred to me. Now that we've got this guy, what the hell are we to do with him?

Before I could think of what to do next, David said, "Lon, I feel like...I feel...I could make strange sounds."

This was a twist. "Let yourself." I told him. "Go with it." I tried to sound calm.

"*Naw-n tahelo hoh athayzo raygayeff*...this is bullshit!"

"No! Relax let it happen!"

"I mean it, I feel like an idiot. I'm too...*zil-zi-anzilzi-lo-da-arp nan-ta*...(inaudible)... *ef*...*efee thar-zi*. I am sorry. That's all. Nothing like this has ever happened before. I just felt like doing it." David's apology was comical. We all broke into nervous giggles.

It had been quite an evening. As we had planned nothing particular to do with LAIDROM I thought it wise to quit while we were ahead. I asked David to thank our spirit guest for his visit and proceeded to banish and close the temple.

One of the class members had brought along his Enochian Dictionary[7] and suggested we try to use it to see if David's strange babbling actually meant something. I rewound the tape and played it back from the beginning. Everything was crystal clear right up to the time of LAIDROM's appearance, when the tape developed an irritating distortion. We joked that it was the fault of malicious spirits and expected it to soon clear up. It did not. In fact by the time the tape reached David's babbling we could hardly pick his voice out from behind the bank of white noise.

---

[7] *The Complete Enochian Dictionary—A Dictionary of the Angelic Language as Revealed to Dr. John Dee and Edward Kelley*, by Donald C. Laycock. First edition (London: Askin Publishers, 1978); most recent edition (York Beach, ME: Samuel Weiser, 1994).

As soon as the good stuff was over the distortion suddenly stopped.

Noise notwithstanding, after replaying the section of tape a dozen times or more we picked up enough of what was being said to write down three audible strings of syllables:

naw-n tahelo hoh athayzo raygayeff.
zil-zi-anzilzi-lo-da-arp nan-ta...(inaudible) and
ef...efee thar-zi.

Starting at the beginning we painstakingly played with the phonetics of each word (and the word/words following) and attempted to match them with words in the Enochian Dictionary. Obviously we weren't being very scientific, nor I confess, very objective. This was all very exciting and romantic and I am sure that night we would have squeezed *some* profundity out of any string of sounds. Be that as it may, it took less than an hour to break the sounds up as follows:

Nanta, elo Hoath zorge ef.—Which translated neatly to: "Spirit of Earth, first worshiper friendly visit."

Zil zien—"Stretch forth hands."
Zilodarp Nanta—"Stretch forth and conquer Spirit of Earth."
Ef etharzi—"Visit in peace."

Needless to say we were all very impressed. At the end of the evening it was agreed that from then on class would meet two times a week to pursue Enochian magick. Sadly, David's ability to break spontaneously into the Enochian language would diminish rapidly as his familiarity with the language of the Calls increased. After the fourth or fifth session he lost the ability completely. His visions, on the other hand, became clearer, more informative, and more provocative.

CHAPTER 21

Enochian Spirits
—ACMBICU

The Enochian Studies class continued twice weekly for nearly three years. During that time David was the primary skryer, but each of us regularly took our turn at the wheel. We systematically worked our way through the spirits of the Elemental Tablets starting with the Seniors,[1] then the Kerubs,[2] then the Servitors.[3]

Early in our work with the planetary Seniors a most extraordinary session took place. Our subject that evening was ACMBICU, Mercury Senior of the Elemental Tablet of Earth. He was only the fourth Senior we had called forth, and his appearance was a shocking departure from those of the previous visions.

Before our first session with ACMBICU each Senior appeared attractively humanoid or even superhuman. ACMBICU imme-

---

[1] Six Seniors per tablet.
[2] Four primary Kerubs per tablet (one governing each subangle).
[3] Sixteen primary Servitors per tablet (four per subangle under the rulership of the primary Kerub).

diately emerged in David's vision as monstrous variation of a great ape. His actions were violent and senseless.

"What is this thing doing?" I asked.

To this day I can still hear David's deep and dramatic voice. "He is squatting down on the ground...and throwing *mud* in his crotch."

All attempts to communicate with ACMBICU were answered by similar obscene and inscrutable gestures. This was hardly the androgynous visage, refined behavior, and eloquent conversation we expected from a spirit of Mercury.

Over and over again I asked the standard set of questions that we developed when working with the other Seniors: What is the nature of your being? What are your duties in nature? How do you manifest in the human heart, the human emotions, in human desires? Have you ever possessed a figure in human history? Have your qualities ever been described as a character in literature that we might recognize?[4] ACMBICU ignored every question.[5]

Eventually his behavior locked in a curious repetitious loop. David described a line of white rocks about the size of footballs laying on the dirt in front of the spirit. ACMBICU then would pick up one rock in his right hand and another rock in his left hand and replace one with the other on the ground. He then did the same thing, replacing the rocks to their original places. This happened over and over again until we gave up, banished the

---

[4] I realize these questions may seem strange and somewhat trivial. We learned early in our Enochian work that we learn nothing from a spirit unless we understand how it executes its specific duties in nature and ourselves. It should be obvious that historic or literary characters are expressions of spirits. When the Venus Senior of the Elemental Tablet of Air tells you she possessed Isadora Duncan, you immediately understand a thousand collateral things about the spirit.

[5] I do recall it telling us that its sacred animal was the armadillo.

temple and called it a night. It was the first time that a session ended in such disappointment. Poor David worried that he might be losing his seership skills the same way he lost the ability to speak Enochian.

After the lights came up and the tea was poured we debriefed like we did every session. David made a quick sketch of

Figure 4. LAIDROM, Mars Senior of the Elemental Tablet of Earth (read right to left) ACMBICU, Mercury Senior of the Elemental Tablet of Earth (read top to bottom).

ACMBICU and we all passed it around and joked about its muddy crotch. I asked David to draw the rocks.

"What's there to draw? They were…rocks!"

He hurriedly drew seven rough circles in a vertical line. Then he drew a double-headed arrow pointing to and from the second and fourth rocks from the top. We scratched our heads and concluded there was no cosmic significance to the drawing or our evening's labor.

As I removed the Elemental Tablet of Earth from the table, I tried to locate ACIMBCU's name written in Enochian on the bottom left vertical arm of the great cross that separates the Tablet in to four equal sections. I couldn't find it. I sat the tablet down and looked more closely. I lettered all my Tablets using Enochian characters that are rather hard to read, especially after a long night. Then the proverbial light bulb went on over my head.

Seven rocks, seven letters in ACMBICU's name. I took the drawing of David's rocks and labeled them A-C-M-B-I-C-U. Then I looked at my Tablet of Earth; A-B-M-C-I-C-U. The coloring on the sides of the C and the B pyramids was exactly alike. When I glued the pyramids to the Tablet I must have carelessly reversed their position and didn't catch my mistake until now.

"Look at this!" I called David and the others over to see my discovery. "No wonder ACMBICU was so screwed up! We weren't talking to ACMBICU we were talking to his perverted cousin ABMCICU …who was kind enough to show us what we were doing wrong!"[6]

---

[6] Shortly after the first ACMBICU session, a friend was kind enough to give me a set of microfilm enlargements of Dee and Kelley's "reformed" tablets. In these later versions of the tablets there are numerous changes in the lettering of the squares. In the reformed versions the Mercury Senior of Earth is spelled AHMLICU.

CHAPTER 22

Enochian Spirits
—EHNB

Of all the Enochian Elemental spirits we contacted during the three-year heyday of the Guild of Enochian Studies,[1] one in particular became the object of repeated and concentrated workings. The spirit is EHNB, the ruling entity of the small but immensely powerful Tablet of Union (Spirit Tablet).

The Tablet of Union is the key to the Enochian Elemental system, just as the quintessential element, Spirit, is the key to the elemental universe. Spirit is the glue that binds the other four elements together to form the building blocks of creation. It is also the barrier that prevents the elements from dissolving into one another and turning the universe into mush. Spirit is always pushing and pulling at the same time. This dual role is expressed in Elemental Magick as two pentagrams—Spirit Active and Spirit Passive.

The Enochian Tablet of Union is actually a simplified and *Macrocosmic* rendition of the four Elemental Tablets.[2] It is made

---

[1] G.O.E.S., the informal name of our little group.
[2] See my *Tarot of Ceremonial Magick* (York Beach, ME: Samuel Weiser, 1995).

Figure 5. The Enochian Tablet of Union.
The letters EHNB rule their respective names and elements,
making EHNB the ruler of the rulers of the Elements.

up of the names of the four great spirits of the elements:
EXARP—great spirit of Air who rules the entire Elemental Tablet of Air; HCOMA—who rules the entire Elemental Tablet of
Water; NANTA—who rules the entire Elemental Tablet of Earth;
and BITOM—who rules the entire Elemental Tablet of Fire. See
figure 5.

These four great spirits rule the entire Elemental universe
and the spirit represented by the first letter of each of their names
(EHNB) rules *the four great spirits!* Anyway you look at it EHNB
is one big spirit in the Enochian system. One side of each of the
four pyramids of its name is attributed to an element (E-Air, H-
Water, N-Earth, B-Fire). The remaining three sides are pure Spirit.
(In other words, the elemental structure of EHNB is a powerful
yet balanced mixture of twelve parts Spirit, one part Air, one part
Water, one part Earth, and one part Fire.)

As a group we avoided the Tablet of Union for nearly a year
because of a comment made by Aleister Crowley in his *Book of
Thoth:*

> *Generally speaking, the attributions of Spirit are not clear
> and simple like those of the other elements. It is very
> remarkable that the Tablet of Spirit in the Enochian sys-*

*tem is the key to all mischief; as, in the Hindu system,
Akasha is the Egg of Darkness.*[3]

He doesn't go on to explain what he means by "...the key to all
mischief..." but it was enough to keep us away from working the
Tablet of Union for a very long time. When we finally got up the
nerve to do it, we were most pleasantly surprised. Fearing "mischief," David and I decided to first do it privately a day or so
before class.

First of all, EHNB is extremely easy to call forth. The temple
opening ceremony is very brief and only the first and second
Calls are intoned. David immediately described a circular temple
setting with circular well in the center of the floor and a domed
ceiling with a circular hole in the top. EHNB in humanoid form
(and dressed rather ostentatiously and wearing an enormous ring)
stood near the well.

I began with the same question I had asked all the Enochian
spirits upon their appearance. "What is the nature of your being?"

It did not answer verbally, but stretched forth its hand, and,
with its finger, pointed to the circumference of the temple floor.
David interpreted. "Its nature is universal."

"What are its specific duties?"

David answered in the first person. "The mechanism of the
universe you understand or can ever understand is contained
within me. I am everything. I do everything. I know everything."

I didn't know what to say. I didn't know what to ask. Finally
I asked David what EHNB was doing now.

"Just standing by the well looking bored."

I wanted time to think. EHNB was more than I was prepared for. I asked David to thank it for coming and ask it if it
would readily appear again for other members of the class if we

---

[3] *The Book of Thoth*, by Aleister Crowley (York Beach, ME. Samuel
Weiser, 1974), p. 177.

called it in the same manner. It agreed. We then bade it farewell and closed the temple.

At the next class David and I did not share the EHNB story with the others. Instead I asked another class member if she would be willing to skry a spirit from the Tablet of Union. Our volunteer was not as skilled as David, nor was she possessed with his rich vocabulary of visual images. Nevertheless, EHNB appeared to her standing before a circular campfire surrounded by a circle of stones. He wore a fringed leather coat and fringed pants. I asked her if she had anything she wished to ask EHNB. She declined, feeling almost intimidated by its presence.

After I banished and closed, David and I related the story of our first EHNB encounter with the other members of the class. Everyone was struck by the similarities of the two visions. We decided for the time being that EHNB would be the focus of our elemental workings.

In the months and years that followed, EHNB proved without question to be the most cooperative and informative spirit in the Enochian elemental system. In my opinion it is the classic spirit guide. One evening, while questioning it on the nature of time, I asked if it was aware of the periods of life and consciousness that we humans view as incarnations. EHNB answered in the affirmative. I then asked if it could show us visions of our previous incarnations. Again the answer was yes.

"Then show me one of mine," I foolishly asked. "Show me how I died."

The seer began to describe an urban scene of what appeared to be a city in the Near East. A young man with a bushy mustache was on the rooftop of a building about two or three stories high. Telegraph poles and lines were in view telling us that we were no farther back in time than the mid-19th century. There was laughter. The young man stepped to the edge of the roof and put his foot on a wire that stretched over the street to another building. He fell. He died. The end.

I want to make it perfectly clear that although I believe in the continuity of existence, I do not hold to the simplistic theory that upon death a vaporous ghost containing our soul floats out of our dead body and goes to some cosmic waiting room while a karmic committee tallies up our unfulfilled needs and desires and matches us up with two unsuspecting fools who deserve the hell that we will put them through as much as we deserve the hell they will put us through. I am very confident, however, in the cycles of nature, and I do not see any reason to believe that the same cyclic behavior we observe in the universe around us cannot apply to *consciousness* and the continuity of our existence. Perhaps, because of the fragile nature of time, we are living all our "incarnations" simultaneously.[4]

That being said, I will remind you that as an infant I had many memories that could be interpreted as stemming from previous incarnations. I confess not one of them, to my recollection, had the remotest semblance to the one described by EHNB on that evening. Be that as it may, in my first year of college I volunteered to be the subject in a study of hypnotic age regression.[5] I was hypnotized by a licensed and experienced hypnotherapist and regressed past infancy to the last moments of a theorized previous incarnation. I was a young man. I had a thick black moustache that I could easily see when I lowered my eyes. I was dressed in loose white pants and a white shirt that was open to my navel. I was on a rooftop looking across to a building of the same height across the street. A wire joined the two buildings. Motivated by a wire-walking act I had recently seen, and urged on by my mischievous friends, I picked up a length of pipe to use as my balancing pole and stepped onto the wire. I fell. I died. The end.

---

[4] This would certainly be the case in a dimensional environment where time is transcended.
[5] This information was not known to the seer.

CHAPTER 23

Enochian Spirits
—A Postscript

As I mentioned before, the Guild of Enochian Studies met twice a week for nearly three years. The lodge grew surprisingly fast and put increasing demands upon my time. Even though I have not resurrected the G.O.E.S. per se, I still make Enochian skrying sessions part of my regular magick class, and encourage even beginning students to learn the basics and start a personal program of exploration.

Today, scholarship on Enochian magick is greater than at any other time in history. Aspects of the system that our little class never even approached are currently the subject of thorough examination and lively discussion. I am thrilled at the conversations I follow on the Enochian "chat" lines and am gratified to see that a new generation of brilliant Enochian magicians is giving this marvelous system the attention it deserves. My personal Enochian work for the last ten years has for the most part been limited to my repeated exploration of the thirty Enochian heavens, or Aethyrs.

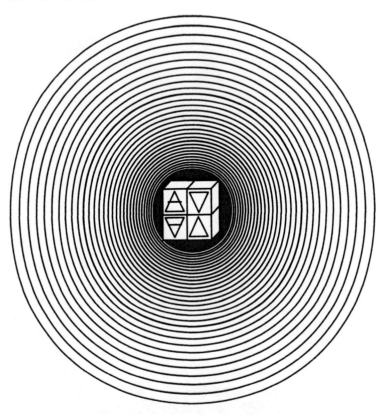

*Figure 6. The thirty heavens, or Aethyrs, of the
Enochian universe surround the four Elemental
Watchtowers in thirty concentric spherees.*

Instead of classifying the material and celestial universe and
the levels of human consciousness in terms of the ten sephiroth
and twenty-two paths of the Qabalistic diagram called the Tree
of Life, Enochian magick sees the world arranged a little differ-
ently. Surrounding the four Elemental Tablets (or watchtowers)
that form the matter and energies of the phenomenal universe,
there are thirty spherical Aethyrs, one enveloping another like
layers of an onion. Like the paths and sephiroth of the Tree of

Life, each Aethyr is reflected in the "software" of the human consciousness matrix.

The qabalistic magician engages in a program of "pathworkings" and systematically explores the paths and sephiroth of the Tree of Life in skrying sessions. It is common, even for beginners, to obtain *some* visions in all levels of the Tree. But, to those who are truthful with themselves, it is always obvious when they have reached a level where their current level of initiation (the highest level of consciousness they can currently achieve) prevents them from obtaining an undistorted vision of that plane.

The Enochian magician explores the thirty Aethyrs in precisely the same manner. Over the years I have systematically skryed all thirty Aethyrs half a dozen times. Each time starts out very strong, the early Aethyrs clear and full of useful information and insights. Then, inevitably, there comes a point where the vision is seen as through a glass darkly. The messages are jumbled and cryptic, the angelic governors unstable and crabby. It is then that I know that I have reached the limit of my personal level of initiation. I must do something with myself and *to* myself to break through to the next higher level of consciousness. More often than not, I find that the key to achieving the next level is to be found in my own diary, in the notes from the last Aethyr I could successfully penetrate.

I confess, I still don't get very far before I hit the "glass darkly" stage. Nevertheless, I feel that by periodically visiting the Aethyrs, no matter how distorted most of them may be, a magician can gain real insight as to his or her personal spiritual progress. Furthermore, unlike qabalistic pathworkings that are often "jump-started" by guided imagery exercises telling the seer what they "should" be seeing at any given point ("In Hod you will meet a man in an orange cloak eating fishsticks with his toes."), the Enochian seer is obliged to view visions that are entirely unique to his or her vocabulary of images.

CHAPTER 24

The Curse of Belial (Never Share a Fiend with a Friend)

Aleister Crowley wrote, "the Single Supreme Ritual is the Attainment of the Knowledge and Conversation of the Holy Guardian Angel. *It is the raising of the complete man in vertical straight line.* Any deviation from this line tends to become black magic. Any other operation *is* black magic...If the Magician needs to perform any other operation than this, it is only lawful insofar as it is a necessary preliminary to That One Work."[1]

The Western magical tradition teaches there are ten major landmarks in the initiate's journey. These of course aren't geographic landmarks; rather, they are ten progressively higher levels of consciousness. Students of Eastern mysticism are quick to point out that at least seven of these landmarks of consciousness correspond nicely with the seven chakras or psychic centers in the human body. Either way you look at it, attainment to the

---

[1] *Magick—Book Four—Liber ABA—Part III—Magick in Theory and Practice,* by Aleister Crowley (York Beach, ME: Samuel Weiser, 1997), p. 275.

next level endows the initiate with greater insight, wisdom, and power.

When Crowley wrote about *Knowledge and Conversation of the Holy Guardian Angel*, he was referring specifically to achieving and maintaining the level of consciousness corresponding to the sixth sephira of the Tree of Life. In Eastern terms, this coincides with the opening of the Anahata chakra (heart, or Christ center) in the human psychic body.

Until the initiate has achieved this level of consciousness, he or she is more or less blind to the true nature of his or her spiritual condition, and therefore ill equipped to make competent magical decisions. The only acts of magick that are lawful before this grade is achieved are those designed to break down obstacles that prevent the magician's magical progress toward that goal.

More often than not, the new magician doesn't have a clue as to what those obstacles really are. Consequently, magical workings at this stage of one's career are a hit and miss affair, and often meet with less than roaring success. So high is the failure rate that many magical instructors forbid their students from dabbling in anything other than the invocation of the Holy Guardian Angel. This, I feel, is a mistake. Unless a few things blow up in your face you will never learn what you will need to do, and *who you will need to become* to avoid such mistakes in the future.

It is true that if I had listened to my teacher before I evoked Orobas for the first time[2] I could have spared myself the agonizing pain of burning my eyes with cinnamon oil. On the other hand, I would have missed the opportunity to learn a score of invaluable magical lessons: I would have denied myself a priceless ego-shattering experience; I might have never have become aware of the various parts of my soul; I might have remained

---

[2] *See* chapters 16 and 17.

completely ignorant of the nature of the spirits, not to mention the possibility that Mad Bob might not have shown up with the car that so dramatically rescued my family from destruction.

I was very lucky with that first evocation. The reason, I believe, that everything worked out was because it was my unambiguous will to pull my life together. I wasn't experimenting. I wasn't praying. I was actually *doing* something for myself. I think I could have done anything—sacrificed a cigar and a bottle of rum—performed an unnatural act with a cheese grater—anything would have worked!

On the other hand, if the object of the operation is not one's unambiguous will, or if your will is divided against itself for one reason or another, the energy you pour into the magick just seems to make things worse. A most dramatic example of such a breech in formula occurred when I tried to share a demon with a friend for the purpose of prospering a business venture.

In 1981, Matt Benton, an old musician friend of mine who had recently earned his Ph.D. in psychology, offered me a job editing a series of books he had written in conjunction with a therapeutic boardgame he had developed in grad school. It was without a doubt the best job I ever had. The pay was good and the work very interesting. It even included a car.

A little less than a month after I started the job, the project was hit with some unforeseen and expensive surprises. A sizable chunk of investment capital had been withdrawn, and unless new cash could be injected into the enterprise, the project (and my job) would have to be postponed.

The only way Matt could quickly raise the needed cash was to secure another loan on his already heavily encumbered home. In desperation he took counsel with an attorney of colorful integrity and together they filed loan paperwork that can only be described as "surreal."

Knowing that I would prefer to keep working, Matt asked if there was anything "magical" I could do to assure that the loan

committee would somehow approve the package without reading it. I figured it was my unambiguous will to keep working so
I foolishly suggested that we enter into a joint evocation of Goetic
spirit.

Matt loved the idea. We thumbed through the text together
and settled on Belial, the 68th spirit of the Goetia, a spirit I had
heretofore not evoked. The text reads:

> BELIAL—He is a Mighty and Powerful King, and was
> created next after Lucifer. He appeareth in the Form of
> Two Beautiful Angels sitting in a Chariot of Fire. He
> speaketh with a Comely Voice, and declareth that he fell
> first from among the worthier sort, that were before
> Michael, and other Heavenly Angels. His office is to dis-
> tribute Presentations and Senatorships, etc., and to cause
> favour of Friends and of Foes. He giveth excellent Fa-
> miliars, and governeth 80 Legions of Spirits. Note well
> that this King Belial must have Offerings, Sacrifices and
> Gifts presented unto him by the Exorcist, or else he will
> not give True Answers unto his Demands. But then he
> tarrieth not one hour in the Truth, unless he be con-
> strained by Divine Power...[3]

Because Belial appears as two spirits, I thought it particularly
appropriate for an operation involving two magicians. I had never
performed a dual evocation before[4] so I was unsure as to the
best way to proceed. I decided Matt and I should operate simultaneously from two different locations (our respective homes). I
set to work making two poster-board triangles and two paper

---

[3] *The Goetia, The Lesser Key of Solomon the King,* trans. Samuel Liddell
MacGregor Mathers, edited, annotated, introduced, and enlarged by
Aleister Crowley. Most recent edition by Hymenaeus Beta (York Beach,
ME: Samuel Weiser, 1995).

[4] I didn't realize at the time that it was the stupidest idea in the world!

Figure 7. Sigil of Goetic Spirit Belial

versions of Belial's sigil. I also engraved the demon's sigil on two copper disks. On the back of each disk I engraved the classic Tetragrammaton Pentagram. These we would wear around our necks during the evocations.

I wrote up two outline rituals. Mine would be the more elaborate version similar to the one I used for the evocation of Orobas and others. Matt's version was very simple and designed primarily to link his temple with mine.

Matt lived less than two miles from my home, so it was very easy for me to go to his house and help him set up his circle and triangle and assure myself that he and his temple were in order. Matt had never done anything like this before and was understandably a little nervous. We cast his circle around a gigantic easy chair in his living room so he could sit comfortably during the ten or fifteen minutes I estimated it would take for the evocation.

Before I left Matt's house I banished the room and consecrated his circle. We briefly reviewed what he was to do in the joint ceremony. It was very simple. After I left he was to take a shower while he repeated the appropriate verse.[5] He was then to put on his bath robe (he didn't have a magical robe) and enter his living room temple. He was to place his paper sigil (which was drawn on the back of a letter signed by one of the bank loan officers) in the triangle and his copper sigil around his neck. Then, for the duration of the specified time

---

[5] See chapter 16 (Evocation of Orobas).

he was to remain in the chair within the circle and repeat a short mantra;

> Belial thou mighty King,
> Accept thou now this offering.
> Send forth your legions to secure,
> The Loan Committee's signature.[6]

Matt was then to wait in the circle until I returned to banish and close his temple.

We synchronized our watches and I rushed home to begin the conjuration at the designated moment. As Belial demands offerings and sacrifices, I decided, with uncharacteristic machismo, that I would initiate the proceedings by scratching the sigil of demon on my left arm with a compass point and then stamping the mark with my blood onto a round piece of parchment. This I placed in the triangle to serve as the material basis for the spirit's manifestation.

My conjuration was accompanied by no strange occurrences whatsoever. Although I didn't actually see the spirit in the triangle, my inner senses all informed me loud and clear that Belial greedily accepted my sacrifice of blood and that the object of our operation would succeed. After giving the spirit his charge, I banished the temple and rushed back to Matt's house.

I found Matt in his black bathrobe sitting in his big easy chair. He seemed a little shaken. I performed the banishing rituals of the pentagram and hexagram, then asked him how it went. He said, "Well...I'm not sure. But I think I'd like to take another shower. Don't sit in that chair."

Matt disappeared into the bathroom and took a quick shower. He returned with a towel and bottle of pine scented disinfectant. Without saying a word he proceeded to thoroughly clean his chair.

---

[6] I know. I know. It's hopelessly corny. I am embarrassed to even write about it. At the time Matt and I thought it was incredibly heavy.

This was very strange. I didn't know if I wanted to know what was going on.

"Let's go get something to eat," he finally said. "My treat."

Over dinner he told me the most remarkable story.

In my first draft of this chapter I wrote down as much as I could remember concerning his story. I read it to Matt to see if there was anything he could add. He said it was fine, but got out his journal of that period just to double check. It was the first time I had ever seen his diary. After reading it I asked him if I he would allow me to reproduce his diary notes instead of using what I had written. He graciously consented. Please excuse his abbreviations and shorthand use of the language. (Compared to some of my diary entries, Matt's notes read like Shakespeare.)

> *7/23—6:30–8:15 p*
> Black magic cer. Demon Belial w/Milo to bewitch for bank loan. Did simul. Milo at his house, me at mine. My part did not go as planned but think it worked. Very strange. See below.
>
> M. strung clothesline circle around my Lazyboy. Inside a cardboard Δ we put a letter signed by _____ from the bank. On the back M. drew magic symbol of Belial.
>
> [hand drawn symbol in diary here]
>
> M. also scratched the same sign on two copper circles for us to wear around our necks. M. vanished *(sic.)* my house before he went home to do his thing. All I to do was shower and "feel holy" and at 6:30 sit in my chair and repeat a poem M. made up—
>
>> Belial thou mighty king, accept thou now this offering.
>> Send forth your legions to secure,
>> the loan committee's signature.
>
> I to stay in chair till he returns back to vanish *(sic.)* my house again. Around 6:10 showered and tried to

read another poem M. wrote for me to say. Got it wet—couldn't read it. I put on bathrobe and tried to put medallion around my neck. The chain got snagged on robe and broke. 6:25 sat down in my chair and tried to relax. Too hot for bathrobe. Took off. Put medallion on the chair between my legs. Sunlight coming in from partially opened front door uncomfortably bright in my eyes. Closed eyes and tried to remember the poem.

Hard to say what happened next b/c so unlike anything that every *(sic.)*

I fell asleep. Sitting up in the chair with the sun in my face. In dream I saw myself reclined in chair with K. naked and astride me like Tues. night. It was so unlike her to make love in the daylight. Great sex, and started to climax, but in back of my mind knew I was supposed to be doing something else. (Note: first wet dream since starting my journals, nearly six years!) I tried to wake up. I was laughing at craziness of whole thing. But I didn't know if I was laughing in dream state or awake. The climax brought me fully conscious. Confused/embarrassed. Chair wet with issue. Medallion covered. Am sure not what M. had in mind for my part of ceremony. Clock read 6:45. M. due back soon to vanish *(sic.)*. I put on my robe and cleaned up the chair as much can *(sic.)* and waited inside the circle for him to return.

I wasn't sure I was going to but I told M. pretty much everything that happened. He thought I was joking at first and said that nothing like that had ever happened to him—told me sounds like I got the good half of the demon.

I was a bit uncomfortable with the sexual component of Matt's experience, especially because it was not part of the original operation. It seemed uncomfortably like an act of spiritual vampirism. Still, I did not share my concerns with Matt because I did not want to throw a wet blanket on his enthusiasm over his first magical operation. Furthermore, three days later we learned that the loan committee had approved the loan and offered an additional fifteen percent if Matt so requested. He so requested. The project was on again.

I need to point out that everything related to the project seemed to carry with it demonic, even dangerous baggage. This is not to say that things didn't go well. On the contrary things seemingly went very well indeed. For example:

We needed an artist, a cartoonist, who could translate Matt's texts into storyboard cells. To retain such a talent for a six to ten month term could understandably be very expensive. We started our quest in Laguna Beach talking with the owners of various studios. As we expected, there was no shortage of talent, but none of it affordable. We ended the first day of our search empty-handed. We stopped at a local saloon (one of the most infernal in town) for a beer and sat down right next to our artist. He was old and bald and smoked cheap cigars. The beard around his mouth was stained ugly yellow from years of cigar smoke. He was obnoxiously drunk.

The bartender started talking about him as if he couldn't hear what he was saying.

"That old goat is Jack Barr. He was the smallest man ever to play football for the Rams. The guy's a cartoonist. Here, look."

The bartender slid a recent issue of *Playboy* down the bar. Sure enough, a Jack Barr cartoon. It was very funny. Not only that but I recognized his style from a score of other *Playboy* cartoons that I had enjoyed over the years. He was for real. He was in front of us. He most likely would work very cheaply. But he was a hopeless drunk and currently in no condition to talk.

The bartender was a wealth of information. He told us the pattern of Barr's life hadn't changed in fifteen years. The alcohol in his blood dictated a strict schedule.

Each morning (Saturdays and Sundays included) at 10:00 A.M. he arrived to "open" his favorite bar. He drank beer, smoked cigars and ate lightly (mostly pickled eggs and burritos) until 5:00 P.M. (when he had to be home to feed his dog). He did what chores he could manage until around 8:00 P.M. when he passed out. He awoke every morning at 3:00 A.M., showered and drank black coffee while he drew in his studio—drew wonderful things; terrible things; little things that he sent out regularly for publication; big things that covered his wall with monstrous specters from his tortured soul.

Matt and I appeared at his home at 5:30 A.M. the next day and talked to him about the project. He was perfectly sober and enthusiastic about the project. We told him what we could pay and he accepted without quibbling.

Old Jack Barr served us well throughout the entire project, but in order for us to exploit his talent, Matt and I were obliged to radically adjust the schedule of our lives to accommodate the old man's nightmarish daily cycle. The three of us met daily at 6:00 A.M. to see the newest drawings and lay out plans for the next night's work. We had to carefully write out every detail of instruction because when Jack woke up at 3:00 A.M. he would be unable to remember the previous day's conversation.

Jack Barr was just one of the "demon" helpers who labored for us on this venture. Each one executed his or her assigned task to our satisfaction, but each also brought with them some vice or infernal flaw that managed to extract from Matt and me some painful measure of personal concession. I am not exaggerating when I say it was truly like working with pack of demons.

Still, the results were impressive. Matt's career was off with a bang. The books were printed. The "game" was manufactured. Matt lectured at a local University and was "discovered" by a newspaper reporter, who splashed his picture and story across the front page of the *Accent* section of the *Sunday Los Angeles Times*. This publicity led to the direct-mail sale of the entire first edition of the books and game, and spawned a dizzying schedule of college lectures.

Our next request for Belial was to remove any obstacles that might prevent Matt from opening his own counseling center. We performed another joint evocation, which, this time, was not accompanied by strange phenomena. As far as we could tell, the operation was also successful, and Matt was soon the director of his psychological counseling center and the darling of the recovery industry.

The center became quite popular. Matt took on two additional associates and the three of them booked a full schedule of clients. Matt also facilitated groups in the evenings and held weekend intensives. The money was good.

My job was done. Matt got everything he wanted and more from our little magick fiend. I got over a year of steady work and a segue to an even better position in commercial real estate. I moved on to my new job and Matt settled into his blossoming career. We both more or less forgot Belial. Neither one of us called him up again to thank him or give him another one of those "offerings" that he likes so well. Matt just went on with his unambiguous magical will to succeed, and my unambiguous will went on to focus on other things. Beliel's joint masters abandoned him, and Matt's fortunes were soon to change.

It all started when Elizabeth, Matt's receptionist and secretary, got married to a client of Matt's, a wealthy entrepreneur named Charles who came to the center to overcome a drug addiction. After they were married, Charles and Elizabeth moved to the Midwest where, for one reason or another, Elizabeth became hopelessly addicted to cocaine. Charles was beside himself and called Matt and made him an offer he could not refuse.

Confident in Matt's discretion and ability to help clients overcome drug problems, Charles offered Matt an exorbitant figure to fly to their home and treat Elizabeth on a twenty-four hour basis until she was clean. He also paid for all lost client fees Matt would incur while he was away. Matt accepted. The treatment took five weeks, during which time Charles confided in Matt the nature of his business. In keeping with the theme of this chapter I need only say that Charles was a creature of the *underworld* and Matt had unwittingly become one of his minions.

Predictably, Charles paid Matt in cash—cash that Matt put in his briefcase for the return flight home—a brief case that was opened by airport officials in the Midwest—airport officials that had questions—questions Matt would not answer.

In all likelihood the authorities realized that Matt was more or less an innocent acquaintance of Charles who was in the wrong place at the wrong time carrying a large amount of questionable cash. Nevertheless, they mistakenly believed Matt could give them useful information concerning Charles' operation, and in order to pressure him to cooperate, they arrested him on a number of charges (none of which included the charges of stupidity and ill-placed loyalty). Bail and subsequent legal fees devastated Matt's finances. He lost his house to foreclosure. As the home loan was the original object of our magical operation I called Matt and told him that it was clear that Belial had turned against the game plan and urged that we exorcise him from our lives. He agreed.

I conjured Belial one last time and gave him license to depart and dismissed him from my service. I then burned his paper sigil and sanded his sign from the copper medallion. I drove to Matt's "new" home on the beach and together we performed a brief exorcism. Instead of sanding down his copper medallion, Matt wanted to destroy it by casting it into the sea where it would quickly corrupt in the salt water.

We stepped to the water's edge. Matt hurled it with a mighty sweep and it shot out to sea like a tiny flying saucer. The sea breeze caught it like a Frisbee and lifted it a few feet higher than its original trajectory. Suddenly, a seagull intercepted the disk in mid air and caught it firmly in its beak. Matt and I couldn't believe what we were seeing. We waved our arms and screamed at the bird hoping it would fly further out to sea and drop it. But it circled back and flew toward Matt's little bungalow. It made a few dips and circles and then dropped the disk in the sand about fifty yards down the beach. We ran to where it appeared to fall and carefully combed the sand, but we could not find it.

For the next year, while he fought one expensive legal battle after another, Matt searched for Belial's sigil. He borrowed a metal detector. He built a screen box. He questioned sunbathers who spread their towels in the vicinity. He never found it.

He did, however, eventually resolve his awful situation. It took five years and all of his resources, but in the end he neither betrayed his clients nor did he go to jail for his silence. He pulled his life and career back together and ran his counseling center for as long as it was his unambiguous will to do so.

There is a magical legend that informs us that King Solomon built the great Temple of God with the supernatural help of demons. Afterward he bound the spirits and imprisoned them in a brass bottle, sealed with a leaden seal, and threw it into a river. One day a fisherman netted the bottle and innocently unleashed the spirits back into the world. Solomon eventually caught all but seventy-two of the little devils and sealed them back up again. The remaining seventy-two are the spirits of the Goetia, including Belial.

A couple of years after Matt's unfortunate adventure, he and his new girlfriend were relaxing on the beach with friends who were visiting from Israel. Matt was playing Frisbee with the 14-year-old son of their guests when the boy reached into the sand and recovered the lost medallion of Belial. Matt still keeps it in his office in a place of honor. The boy's name was Solomon.

CHAPTER 25

Andromalius

As I mentioned earlier, I believe that the complexes of natural energy and intellegence that can be personified as "spirits of the Goetia" reside deep within the magician's animal soul (Nephesh). The key to successfully isolating and redirecting these "spirits" lies in our ability to balance and integrate the other parts of the soul to such a degree that these unruly rascals find it easier to cooperate with the magician's game plan than to resist it. This is a very personal thing. Obviously, it was a terrible idea for Matt and I to engage in a dual conjuration of a goetic spirit. A slave cannot serve two masters. As soon as I formally withdrew from the operation, Matt and Belial (the only "two" who should have ever been operating in the first place) became focused on the job at hand and eventually triumphed.

Ever since then I have resisted the temptation to stick my nose into someone else's magical business. However, from time to time friends or acquaintances come to me seeking magical solutions to everyday problems. The best that I can do is to counsel them as to how I might magically proceed in the same situa-

Figure 8. Sigil of Goetic Spirit Andromalius

tion. I can never be sure that my advice is correct because I have no way of knowing another person's karmic profile or the depth of their commitment to the operation.

A few years after my experience with Belial, two of our dearest friends, Pat and Terry, bought the most beautifully appointed Volkswagen camper. They were wildly generous with it and seized any excuse to take Constance and me and other lodge members on road trips, campouts, baseball games, and mini-vacations. Then, less than two months after buying it, the new van was stolen from the parking lot of a movie theater.

The police held out no hope of its recovery. Pat and Terry lived less than sixty miles from the Mexican border, and it was likely that the car was out of the country before they came out of the theater and discovered it missing. We were all heartbroken. Just out of frustration and outrage I wanted to evoke Andromalius,[1] who brings back stolen things. But then I remembered my experience with Belial and reconsidered. I did, however, instruct Pat how he might easily evoke Andromalius.

Pat was not very enthusiastic about performing that kind of magick and I was sure that a half-hearted effort would fail. Pat

---

[1] *The Goetia, The Lesser Key of Solomon the King,* trans. Samuel Liddell MacGregor Mathers, edited, annotated, introduced, and enlarged by Aleister Crowley. Most recent edition by Hymenaeus Beta (York Beach, ME. Samuel Weiser, 1995). *"...He is an Earl, Great and Mighty, appearing in the Form of a Man holding a Great Serpent in his Hand. His Office is to bring back both a Thief, and the Goods which be stolen; and to discover all Wickedness, and Underhand Dealing; and to punish all Thieves and other Wicked People; and also to discover Treasures that be Hid. He ruleth of 36 Legions of Spirits..."*

performed some kind of conjuration of Andromalius (he never told me exactly what he did) and gave the spirit two weeks to recover the car.

To everyone's surprise, the car was recovered exactly two weeks later at the Mexican border—the thieves had taken it to Mexico and were trying to cross back into the United States with a shipment of contraband parrots. Andromalius was a hero.

A few days later I told the story to the accountant at work who immediately demanded that I tell her how to whip up Andromalius. Her sister's car had just been stolen by her ex-husband. I sketched out the spirit's sigil and gave her a crash course in Solomonic evocation. The next morning she related to me how she drew a chalk circle and triangle on the floor of her garage and stood in the circle with a bottle of tequila and screamed curses at her former brother-in-law in the form of the sigil of Andromalius in the triangle. That night when I left work she greeted me in the parking lot in her sister's recovered car (a VW van) and rewarded me with a big kiss and a gift box of *Boodles British Gin* (my favorite).

Since then, I have "given" Andromalius to four other individuals for the return of their stolen automobiles.[2] He hasn't failed yet—and I am at a loss to explain why. In my opinion none of these people even came near plumbing the infernal depths of their Nephesh Hells to harness the blind power of their personal demons.[3] Their stolen cars, while a painful loss,

---

[2] One person didn't even get a chance to evoke him. She left our house in a cab with Andromalius' sigil drawn on the back of an envelope. When she returned home her car (a VW bus) was waiting for her in her driveway.

[3] Constance evoked Andromalius to recover a large box of vitamins and other motherly gifts which she sent at great expense to our son in Japan. I had no doubts that "Andy" would comply to a mother's wrath, especially when the nourishment of the baby bird is at stake. Sure enough, the box showed up in Japan. All our subsequent shipments bear the sigil of Andromalius conspicuously displayed front and back.

presented more of an inconvenience than gut-wrenching out-rage. Most of them, to my knowledge, merely went through the motions of standing for a moment in a circle and making a wish at a paper sigil in a triangle. Why did it work? Is Andromalius that easy to enlist? Is he that cooperative?

I feel I must apologize to the reader because I have no clean explanation for this spirit's behavior. It runs counter to my magical field theory about what these spirits are and how they operate. The only thing I can say is this. If your car gets stolen and you want it back (especially if it is a VW bus)—it sure couldn't hurt to evoke Andromalius.

CHAPTER 26

Attack of Aunt Gladys' Ghost

I am often asked if I have ever been attacked personally by a spirit. People are disappointed if I can't terrorize them with some tale of spiritual mayhem. Alas, I have to tell you that (with the exception of my first evocation of Orobas when it was more a case of my own stupidity than the malice of the spirit) I have never been attacked by any spirit that I have formally evoked. I was, however, nearly killed by a spirit I didn't evoke.

Crime statistics show that if you are going to be murdered, it will most likely be by a family member. This is obviously also the case in the spirit world.

As you may recall from chapter two, my Aunt Gladys lived nearly her entire life in Wallace, NE. Her story is one of tragedy and triumph. Crippled at an early age, with a disease that virtually gelatinized her bones, she bravely overcame the harsh cruelties of prairie life to become one of the most beloved and respected matriarchs of her community. She was charming. She was witty. All who came near her immediately found themselves willing slaves of her charisma. Through pure will and strength of character she transformed her wheelchair into a throne from which she dictated the lives of all within her gravitational field.

Her favorite servants were little boys—neighbor boys—relatives—it didn't matter. I can't recall ever seeing her without a tiny footman tirelessly running errands, emptying her chamber pot, and doing a thousand household chores. When they grew older she allowed them to drive her to the outermost reaches of her queendom. While we were living with her, she even attempted to recruit Marc and me into her service, but years of self-centered laziness made us poor candidates for martyrdom.

Please do not misunderstand me, Aunt Gladys was a good woman. She didn't have a malicious gelatinized bone in her body. She did what she had to do and she did it with great style. Nevertheless, it remains a sad fact that many of the dear souls she dominated docilely allowed their lives and personalities to be drained of any semblance of independence or will. Her little boys eventually grew older, but few, it can be said, grew to manhood. Without her dynamic direction many of them drifted into lives of tragic loneliness.

One summer, about a year before she died, Gladys traveled to California for a visit. Constance suggested that we take her to the Huntington Library and Botanical Gardens in San Marino. I heartily agreed. Since Jean-Paul was old enough to walk, we visited the gardens regularly and pretended we lived there. It is one of the most beautiful places on earth; one hundred and forty-four acres of magnificent grounds—pine forest, Japanese garden, Shakespearean garden, fish and turtle ponds, Greek gardens, massive rose arbors, herb gardens and the world's most extensive desert garden. It's paradise—and all of it accessible by wheelchair.

As we predicted, Gladys loved the Huntington gardens. It was a thrill just watching her prairie-parched eyes drink in the exotic colors and forms. Jean-Paul was our guide and I, of course, pushed the wheelchair. Gladys was visibly affected. Several times during the day, she made us stop so she could reach up and hug my neck and tell me it was the happiest day of her life.

By afternoon the temperature reached 103 degrees and I was beginning to tire. We unwisely saved the desert garden for last. It is located in the lowest section of the grounds and the way out is an uphill ordeal even when one is not pushing a wheelchair. By the time we reached the parking lot, Jean-Paul and I each suffered heat stroke. He threw-up and I broke out in a cold sweat, which I couldn't bring under control for several hours. Gladys was in bliss. It would be the last time I saw her alive.

We knew Gladys was pleased with her day at the Huntington, but we had no idea just how pleased she was. She called us as soon as she returned to thank us again. She cried on the phone. We soon heard from other relatives that it was all she could talk about. She made multiple copies of all the photographs from that day and sent them with detailed descriptions to everyone she knew. She gave me all the credit for the happiest day of her life, and told everyone I almost died in the process. After all these years, Lonnie had become her favorite boy.

On the night she died, nearly twenty hours before I would learn of her death, Gladys came to me in a frightening vision. I dreamed I was in her old house in Wallace lying on my back in her great mahogany bed. It was here the dear woman used to let me sit with her for a few minutes at bedtime and she would read to me the funny paper adventures of Dondi and Alley Oop.

This night she was not in the bed. She was standing in the doorway to her bedroom—standing upright without cane or crutches or braces. She slowly walked to the head of the bed. I was so surprised, I said, "Aunt Gladys, you can walk!" She didn't say a word, but reached toward me and pulled the pillow from under my head and placed it gently over my face. I tried to push it off, but my hands and arms were paralyzed. I tried to scream but I could not get any air to come out of my throat. I was suffocating. I tried to thrash my body from side to side but I couldn't tell whether or not I was really moving. I think I managed to let out an awful groan, but I could not articulate any words. I groaned again and struggled against the pillow. I heard Constance's voice telling me to "Breathe! Lon! You're not breathing! Wake up!" I stared wide-eyed into the pillow until it dissolved and I saw the familiar shadows of my own bedroom ceiling. Constance pushed me sharply and yelled again for me to breathe. Finally I found the control to drag in a deep breath and then another.

It was a clear case of sleep apnea. It had happened before. I snore like Godzilla. This was the first time, however, that it had been accompanied by such a strange and terrifying dream.

"I dreamed Aunt Gladys was trying to suffocate me with a pillow." Constance and I both laughed. Still, I would not put my head back down on the spot where the dream had occurred. I spent the rest of the night on the living-room couch. The following evening my brother called to tell us that Aunt Gladys had died the night before.

A few days later my mother flew to Nebraska for her sister's funeral. She stayed for a week afterward to help Gladys' daughter with the disposition of some of her things. Mom brought back a handful of memorabilia to divide between my brother and me. My inheritance was wrapped in tissue and delivered in a large shopping bag. A lovely card from her daughter accompanied it. She wrote to tell me again that Gladys' trip to the Huntington was the happiest moment of her life and that she hoped I would always think of her mother whenever I looked at the silken pillow that Gladys hand embroidered just for me.

CHAPTER 27

How to End an Autobiography Without Dying

And now I am faced with the awkward task of ending an autobiography while still alive. I certainly do not intend to die anytime soon just to provide a clean ending, but as I conclude this little book it might not be a bad idea to pause for a moment to ponder *that undiscovered country from whose bourne no traveler returns* and share with you my thoughts on death.

Do I believe in an afterlife? Do I believe in karma and reincarnation? Do I believe in heaven or hell? Am I afraid to die? The answer to all these questions is a *qualified* "Yes."

On the other hand, if you ask me if I believe that when I die I will be hauled into some celestial courtroom to appear before the God of Judgment who will convict me on evidence of my failure in life to sacrifice my intelligence and common sense in order to believe unquestioningly in a particular cult's interpretation of the details surrounding an historical or mythological event, and/or my inability, or disinclination to submit to a particular collection of ancient superstitions and tribal taboos, then my answer is an *unqualified* "No!"

I am perpetually amazed that stable, intelligent people—people with driver's licenses and college degrees—people who can finish the New York Times crossword puzzle and run huge corporations—people who otherwise display the most superior powers of intelligence and insight can actually look me in the eye and tell me in deadly earnest that they believe:

• That all human beings have been cursed by the creator of the universe because of the very fact that we were born;

• That, because we are already guilty of committing life, the creator has condemned us to eternal torture after we die;

• That we can plea bargain ourselves out of this fate by perfectly surrendering to certain mental and behavioral parameters that are outlined in a book composed of sixty-six chapters written over a period of hundreds of years by an unknown number of authors in an assortment of languages—an unerring book that has been translated scores of times by individuals employed by intensely biased institutions;

• That after we die our corpses (at some unspecified date in the future) will reanimate like zombies and fly up from our graves and hover in the sky at the side of our deity who, sitting on a flying horse, will slaughter one third of the population of the planet. Afterward, this same deity will preside over the ultimate kangaroo court in the clouds and issue one-way tickets to the lake of fire to the newly murdered and all others who in life did not unquestionably believe that all this was the only spiritual game plan in town.

I am sorry my friends. I cannot see how blindly accepting the above doctrine (or any of a hundred others just as ludicrous) could possibly be good for one's mental health. As a matter of fact, it appears obvious to me that in order for a rational, intelligent person to subscribe to such silliness and still live a relatively normal life, he or she must set aside a small corner of the brain devoted exclusively to religious mental illness, and visit that area as infrequently as possible.

This does not mean that I think that individuals who fervently believe in a specific after-death scenario do not experience their expectations in the mysterious timeless moments of the death coma. On the contrary, I think it highly likely that one's visions at the moment of death mirror, in perhaps nightmarish detail, the crystallized "reality" of whatever spiritual worldview has captured and enslaved the decedent's imagination in life.

For this reason, I am particularly saddened when I think of the untold millions of my fellow human beings who have exited this plane of existence still harboring tortuous doubts as to their worthiness to pass such an impossible judgment. Shouldn't religion be satisfied with terrorizing their devotees into social and economic obedience during life? Is it really necessary to demand from these pour souls one last act of tragic self-condemnation insidiously designed to trigger horrifying visions and unspeakable terror during the death experience?

In 1954, I was 6 years old and loved to listen to the radio. That year one of my favorite songs was Rosemary Cloony's "This Ole House."[1] The refrain went something like:

> *Ain't a-gonna need this house no longer*
> *Ain't a-gonna need this house no more*
> *Ain't got time to fix the shingles*
> *Ain't got time to fix the floor*
> *Ain't got time to oil the hinges*
> *Nor to mend the windowpane*
> *Ain't a-gonna need this house no longer*
> *I'm a-gettin' ready to meet the saints*

It's a perky little tune and I didn't give the words much thought until my mother was sensitive enough to point out that the *house* in the song was really someone's body and they were singing about getting ready to die. From then on the song gave me the creeps and I never sang it again. I still can't stand the song, but it makes a very good point. We are not bodies possessing souls. We are souls inhabiting bodies.

---

[1] *This Old House*, written by Stuart Hamblen. Copyright © 1954 Hamblen Music, renewed. Used by permission. Music available from Hamblen Music Co, Box 1937, Canyon Country, CA 91386.

For thousands of years the great Osirian religion of ancient Egypt impressed upon devotees an image of a resurrected body as the key to overcoming death. Changing only a few names and images, Christianity inherited the Osirian formula and has perpetuated it through the 20th century. The Osirian formula is based on the incorrect assumption that the sun is born and dies every day and teeters toward extinction every winter. The identity of the Osirian devotee was centered in Earth—an Earth that just sits in place, a helpless spectator of the sun's birth and death. This is precisely the role played by the pious Christian who can only hope to overcome death by riding the magical coattails of Christ's death and resurrection—a body hoping to come to life again.

Times have changed. We know now that the sun does not die, neither does it need a magical resurrection. Shouldn't it be logical that the next step in spiritual evolution would be to harmonize with our most recent understanding of reality? It's not so hard to move our identity from Earth to the sun. The sun is on all the time. We are on all the time. There is no life after death—only life. I knew it as an infant. That is why I could never picture myself off. The solution to my crib meditation is the simple fact that there is no off.

The body is bound to wear out. Sooner or later there won't be time to fix the shingles, won't be time to fix the floor. Is it such a catastrophe to leave a house that is falling apart? Perhaps the vision I received when I was hypnotically regressed in college and the vision of the Enochian spirit EHNB were not pictures of an actual event, but an allegory of all death experiences.

I wouldn't be a bit surprised if one day, when I am incredibly old and trying to recover from a long afternoon of flamenco dancing and unbridled sex, I close my eyes and find myself standing on the roof of my house. In front of me I see a wire strung tightly to the house across the street. I hear my friends laughing. Once again the sum total of my life's momentum urges me onward toward new experiences—urges me on to the narrow wire that joins *this ole house* to the new one just across the street.

Epilogue:
Holy Man?

I turned 50 on Saturday. I spent the morning writing, and in the afternoon made a half-hearted attempt to clean up my office. Constance, bless her heart, spent the whole day getting our home ready for an invasion of out-of-town guests who will be arriving in a few days to take their O.T.O. Fifth Degree. Last night, my Monday night magick class marked my half centennial with homemade ice cream and cream puffs. There was much laughter and wonderful cards and gifts. I can't deny it, I am a very lucky man. I am surrounded by good spirits.

Now that I think about it, I've always been surrounded by good spirits—spirits who execute their various charges on my behalf through the human vehicles of friends, family, business associates, and even strangers. By the same token, it is clear that I am also surrounded by "evil" spirits who tirelessly labor with diabolic tenacity to effect my ultimate undoing. Ironically these devils also manifest through the human vehicles of friends, family, business associates, and complete strangers.

Please don't think that I am so presumptuous as to actually believe that all these people are actually *possessed* with objective entities that are the angels or demons of Lon Milo DuQuette. On the contrary, it is painfully obvious to me that all the spirits are my own children, creatures of my unique and personal magical universe. Everyone else on the planet has their own magical universe, and I am sure there are a great many people for whom

*Bishops Lon and Constance DuQuette celebrating the
Mass of the Gnostic Catholic Church.*

Lon Milo DuQuette assumes the role, from time to time, of good
or evil spirit.

I continue to do my best to identify and capture my "evil"
spirits and redirect their destructive energy toward constructive
ends. It is the magician's great work and my spiritual occupa-
tion. Sometimes I succeed. Sometimes I fail. Eliphas Levi put it
perfectly in a stanza of his poem, "The Magician":

Their faces and their shapes are terrible and strange,
These devils by my might to angels I will change.

These nameless horrors I address without affright:
On them will impose my will, the law of light.[1]

At the beginning of this book, I acknowledged without apology that I have scorned and rejected the faith of my fathers; that I invoke and worship strange and terrible gods; that I summon devils and hold congress with angels, spirits, and demons. I also asked whether or not these pursuits disqualify me for a place in the august fellowship of the holy ones. In the absence of a tantrum-throwing god of judgement, I guess the only person who can answer that question is yours truly.

Do I think that I am a holy man?

Sometimes.

---

[1] *The Magician*, translated from Eliphas Levi's version of the famous Hymn, in *The Equinox Vol. 1 (1)* (London: Spring, 1909); Reprint York Beach, ME: Samuel Weiser, 1992), p. 109.

Bibliography

Cassabon, Meric. *A True and Faithful Relation of What Passed For Many Years Between Dr. John Dee and Some Spirits.* London: Askin, 1994. Reprint, with introduction by L. M. DuQuette: New York: Magickal Childe Publishing, 1992.

Crowley, Aleister. *The Book of Thoth: A Short Essay on the Tarot of the Egyptians.* The Master Therion. London: O.T.O., 1944, *The Equinox III(5).* Facsimile edition: York Beach, ME: Samuel Weiser, 1991.

———. *The Confessions of Aleister Crowley.* Abridged edition: John Symonds and Kenneth Grant, eds. London: Jonathan Cape, 1969; Reprinted; London: Arkana, 1989.

———. *Crowley on Christ.* First published in typewritten form as a limited edition of 200 copies as *The Gospel According to St. Bernard Shaw*, 1953. Rev. 2nd edition: Francis King, ed. London: Neville Spearman, 1972.

———. *Eight Lecture on Yoga.* Mahatma Guru Sri Paramahansa Shivaji. London: O.T.O., 1939. The Equinox III (4). Rev. 2nd edition: Hymenaeus Beta, ed. Scottsdale, AZ: New Falcon Publications, 1991; New York: 93 Publishing, 1992.

———. *The Equinox Vol. I (1).* London: Spring, 1909. Reprint: York Beach, ME: Samuel Weiser, 1992.

———. *Gems From the Equinox: Instructions by Aleister Crowley for His Own Magical Order.* Israel Regardie, ed. Most recent edition: Scottsdale, AZ: New Falcon Publications, 1992.

———, ed. *The Goetia of Solomon the King.* Samuel Liddel MacGregor Mathers, tr. Foyers, UK: Society for the Propagation of Religious Truth, 1904. New edition with engraved illustrations of the spirits by M. L. Breton and foreword by Hymenaeus Beta. York Beach, ME: Samuel Weiser, 1995.

———. *Magick • Book Four • Liber ABA.* Hymenaeus Beta, ed. York Beach, ME: Samuel Weiser, 1993.

————. *The Qabalah of Aleister Crowley.* York Beach, ME: Samuel Weiser, 1973. Retitled *777 and Other Qabalistic Writing of Aleister Crowley* in the fifth printing, 1977. Reprinted York Beach, ME: Samuel Weiser, 1990.

DuQuette, Lon Milo. *The Magick of Thelema; A Handbook of the Rituals of Aleister Crowley.* York Beach, ME: Samuel Weiser, 1993.

————. *Tarot of Ceremonial Magick.* York Beach, ME: Samuel Weiser, 1995.

DuQuette, Lon Milo, with Christopher S. Hyatt. *Aleister Crowley's Illustrated Goetia.* Scottsdale, AZ: New Falcon Publications, 1992.

DuQuette, Lon Milo, with Aleister Crowley and Christopher S. Hyatt. *Enochian World of Aleister Crowley.* Scottsdale, AZ: New Falcon Publications, 1991.

Goodwin, C. W., tr. *A Fragment of a Graeco-Egyptian Work upon Magic from a Papyrus in the British Museum.* Cambridge: Deighton; Macmillan; London: J. W. Parker; Oxford, 1852.

James, William. *The Varieties of Religious Experience.* London: Longmans, 1910.

Jones, Charles S. (Frater Achad). *Q.B.L. or The Bride's Reception.* Most recent edition, Kila, MT: Kessinger, 1992.

Laycock, Donald C. *The Complete Enochian Dictionary—A Dictionary of the Angelic Language as Revealed to Dr. John Dee and Edward Kelley.* First edition: London: Askin, 1978. Most recent edition: York Beach, ME: Samuel Weiser, 1994.

Lao Tzu. *Tao Te Ching.* C. H. John, tr. Boston: Shambalah, 1990.

Leary, Timothy, with Alan Watts, et al, eds. *Psychedelic Review,* New York: University Books, 1965.

Mathers, S. L. , ed. and tr. *The Kabbalah Unveiled.* London: Keagan Paul, Trench & Trubner, 1887: Reprinted: York Beach, ME: Samuel Weiser, 1993.

————. *The Key of Solomon the King.* London: Redway, 1889; Reprinted: York Beach, ME: Samuel Weiser, 1972, 1992.

Ramacharaka, Yogi (William Walker Atkinson). *Fourteen Lessons in Yogi Philosophy.* Chicago: Yogi Publications, 1931.

————. *The Science of Breath.* Chicago: Yogi Publications, 1931.

Regardie, Israel. *The Golden Dawn.* St. Paul: Llewellyn, 1992.

Runyon, Carroll (Poke). *The Magick of Solomon.* Pasadena, CA: The Church of the Hermetic Sciences, 1996.

Simon, M., and H. Sperling, trs. *The Zohar.* New York: Bennet, 1959.

Suares, Carlo. *The Sepher Yetsira.* Micheline and Vincent Stuart, trs. Boston: Shambalah, 1976.

Index

About the Author

In the dark and brooding firmament of magical literature, Lon Milo DuQuette is a star of unique and exceptional brilliance. Although he takes the subject of ceremonial magick very seriously, he tries to remember not to take himself too seriously. This rare combination of common sense and humor has in the last ten years secured him a respected position in the world of modern occultism.

Since 1975 he has served as a national and international officer of Ordo Templi Orientis, one of the most influential magical societies of the 20th century. He is an acknowledged authority on the life and magick of the O. T. O.'s most celebrated member, Aleister Crowley. His landmark work, *The Magick of Thelema: A Handbook of the Rituals of Aleister Crowley* (Weiser, 1993), is considered a classic in its field, and has been hailed as the first useful primer for Thelemic ritual magick.

However, DuQuette does not confine himself to the Thelemic genre. He travels extensively and speaks on a broad range of esoteric topics including Qabalah and the tarot. He is the creator of *Tarot of Ceremonial Magick* (cards from U.S. Games, book from Weiser, 1995) and is a Certified Grand Master of the American Tarot Association.

In his most recent work, *Angels, Demons & Gods of the New Millennium: Musings on Modern Magick* (Weiser, 1997), DuQuette departed from the textbook format of his previous works and presented a series of critically acclaimed essays and anecdotes of his personal experiences as a practicing magician. *My Life with the Spirits* continues in this vein, offering the reader a biographical sketch of the fascinating, sometimes terrifying, sometimes hilarious, world of a 20th century magician.